RISK FINANCING

Second Edition

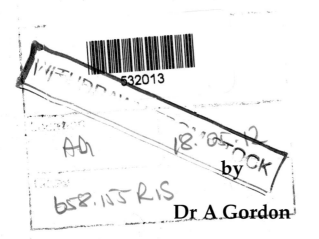

by

Dr A Gordon

OTHER BOOKS IN THE SERIES

Business Finance for Risk Management
Business Organisation and Finance
Corporate Risk Management
Insurance, Non Marine – An Introduction
Liability Exposures
Liability Risk and the Law
Local Government a Text for Risk Managers
Risk Control
Risk and the Business Environment
Risk Analysis
Risk Management in Healthcare
Treasury Risk Management

British Library Cataloguing in Publication Data
Gordon, Dr A
Risk Financing – 2nd Ed.
1 Title
ISBN 1 85609 261 5

Notice of Terms of Use

The Institute of Risk Management
6, Lloyd's Avenue
London EC3N 3AX
www.theirm.org
Tel No: 020 7709 9808

1st Edition 1992
2nd Edition 2003

WITHERBYS
PUBLISHING

© The Institute of Risk Management

2003

ISBN 1 85609 261 5

Published and Printed by
WITHERBY & CO. LTD
32-36 Aylesbury Street
London EC1R 0ET
Tel No: 020 7251 5341   Fax No: 020 7251 1296
International Tel No: +44 20 7251 5341
International Fax No: +44 20 7251 1296
E-mail: books@witherbys.co.uk
www: witherbys.com

Introduction

Corporate governance and risk management have developed rapidly in the past decade as codes of practice, Stock Exchange requirements and indeed corporate failures have all brought pressure on boards of directors to promote improved risk management practices. The Risk Management Standard, launched by IRM in October 2002, sets out a coherent risk management process that requires careful assessment of risks and consequent decisions on how to finance the costs of risk.

Most organisations use insurance as a central tool in alleviating shocks to the balance sheet and interruptions to cashflow. However, directors need to ensure that the levels and type of cover along with its price (the premiums) are compatible with the organisation's wider attitude to risk and financial resources. Risk managers and their advisers are now employing more formal methods for risk analysis and the efficient use of risk financing mechanisms is a key feature of financial management

Alan Gordon's book has been a valuable reference source on risk financing since the first edition was published in 1992. Andrew Tunnicliffe and his colleagues at Marsh have done an excellent job in revising, updating and extending the book to form this edition. The new work covers the fundamentals in detail and expands the analysis of the options in risk financing to include guidance on risk retention decision making, modern uses of the well establish concept of captive insurance companies and Alternative Risk Financing.

The book will be invaluable to both experienced risk management professionals and students alike.

Paul Howard,
Head of Group Insurances and Risk Management,
J. Sainsbury plc
Chairman, IRM 2002-03
August 2003

Contents

1

THE NATURE OF RISK FINANCING

1.1 INTRODUCTION

The student handbook of the Institute of Risk Management defines risk management as the "identification, measurement, control, financing and transfer of risks which threaten the life, property and viability of business enterprises". The importance of this function has grown with the development in the scale and costs of risk faced by organisations. (Corporate governance, Turnbull & Higgs have all added weight to the importance of risk management function within the boardroom.) Expenditure on insurance has risen to the extent that major companies with multi-million pound premium costs are no longer content to leave the management of these funds to relatively junior staff or to a part-time function. The aftermath created by the catastrophic events of 11th September 2001 along with several high-profile company insolvencies has exacerbated this situation, elevating the importance of both risk management and risk financing functions upon the corporate agenda.

The process of risk management is divided into three stages, namely analysis, control and financing. Once a risk has been identified and its significance measured the organisation has to determine the most effective manner of handling the risks concerned. The range of generally recognised options are summarised in Figure 1.1.

Fig 1.1

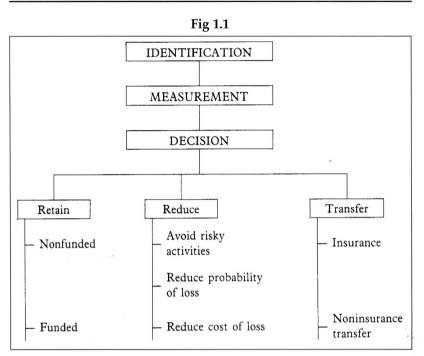

The Recognised Options of Risk

The decision to retain, transfer or reduce risk involves two different types of financial function, namely financing and investment. Investment is concerned with the application of funds and the ensuing return from their deployment; for example in loss prevention and reduction expenditure or the replacement of assets or funds 'destroyed' by a pure loss event.

Financing is concerned with the sources and costs of funds obtained for these expenditures. It is this latter form of financial function that has largely been the focus of risk financing techniques. These techniques have been developed to meet the cost of losses which occur even after the application of the earlier stages of the risk management process – although hopefully these are less than they would otherwise have been!

The main risk financing options are:

- transfer of the risk or financial responsibility for the risk to a third party, contractually;

- retain financial responsibility for the risk;

- transfer financial responsibility for the risk to an insurer;

- a combination of insurance transfer and retention.

Although risk financing has long been identified with insurance, it is by no means the sole or optimum risk financing technique available. It may be more advantageous for the risk to be financed wholly or in part by the organisation. A cost-effective risk financing programme would be likely to involve a mix of financing techniques.

1.2 THE ROLE OF RISK FINANCING

The role of risk financing is to ensure the economic provision of funds to finance the recovery of the organisation from property damage, liability damages, business interruption and personnel losses. Thus it involves:

- evaluation of total values at risk from each class of exposure;

- estimation of total costs of loss within a specified time period (usually an accounting year) together with the maximum severity of any one loss;

- identification of appropriate sources of funding in advance of the loss;

- appraisal of the economic viability of the replacement or repair of assets subject to loss;

- arrangements for securement of these funds in event of loss; and

- direction and control of the use of the funds upon the occurrence of the loss.

1.2.1 The Cost of Risk

The cost of risk to an organisation has been defined by the Risk and Insurance Management Society (RIMS) of New York as total annual expenditures on:

- retained losses;

- insurance premiums;

- risk control and handling costs; and

- risk management administration expenses.

This definition is used by RIMS for its biennial Cost-of-Risk Survey. As it has not yet been universally accepted, definition of the term 'cost of risk' should be checked.

1.2.1.1 The Costs of Losses

The total cost of losses retained if a risk materialises is made up of direct and indirect costs. Direct costs are generally relatively straightforward to identify and include:

- those incurred in repairing or replacing damaged property; and/or

- payment of damages in respect of liability exposures such as employers, public or product.

The indirect costs are more difficult to trace and in many instances exceed the direct costs. Indirect costs would include: business interruption costs; loss of market share; increased insurance premiums; loss of image in the event of product liability claims; the costs of recalling faulty products; loss of production in event of employee injury; management time investigating employee injuries; other expenses relating to employee injuries including medical expenses and paid absence from work.

An important feature in the management of the cost of losses is that the scale of risk has increased giving rise to greater potential loss severities. This is due to a number of interdependent factors such as:

- increased complexities of production processes;

- increased concentrations of asset values;

- internationalisation of the manufacturing process;

- growth in technological interdependence;

- changes in production methods;

- globalisation of markets;

- growth in social awareness of environmental and other issues.

A further consequence of many of these is the rate at which change occurs. Since risk and uncertainty are a function of change, more change implies a greater incidence of risk. The outcome of rapid change and greater values at risk is a rise both in the severity and aggregate costs of losses.

1.2.1.2 The Costs of Controlling or Handling Risk

The costs of handling risk include risk control expenditure and the costs of employing various risk financing devices. Risk financing costs should be distinguished from the cost of losses.

Risk control expenditure covers a diverse range of devices and procedures designed to prevent or reduce the frequency of occurrence. Examples include: machine guards; protective clothing; safe operating procedures; safety audits; training; fire and intruder alarms; strong rooms; fencing; security guards; fire extinguishers; duplication of records; and stand-by plant and services to reduce the period of interruption to operations.

Risk financing devices include: insurance; the use of internal cash resources or reserves; credit facilities such as lines of credit; captive insurance companies; and pre-loss and post-loss alternative risk financing structures which often provide a blending of risk financing and risk transfer.

These devices are employed by risk managers in pursuit of the preservation of corporate or community assets. This is illustrated in the example of Paper Clip plc below.

1.2.2 Paper Clip plc

Paper Clip plc is a relatively young company at the forefront of a new technology with a potential for rapid market growth. It is expected to grow from its present net worth of £10m at a rate of 30% per annum over the next ten years. Under this assumption the value of the company at the end of the tenth year would be £137.86m. This projection however has ignored the existence of pure risk.

The effect of introducing pure risk in the form of "random losses" on the value of the company is shown graphically by line AB in Figure 1.2. The contrast with the "no loss" scenario (line AA) is evident.

Fig 1.2

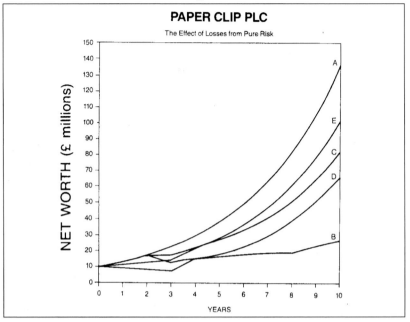

PAPER CLIP PLC
The Effect of Losses from Pure Risk

The Random Loss and No Loss Scenario

The reduction in the value of the company is due in part to the fact that no financial provision has been made to replace the assets subject to loss when these occur. The company therefore has to absorb the loss from its own resources, diverting these where necessary from productive use.

A number of steps can be taken to reduce the effect of these losses. In this example we will consider three options:

    (i) introduce loss controls but with no provision for replacement of lost assets;

    (ii) buy insurance but without loss controls;

    (iii) operate loss control methods and buy insurance.

Loss control

Assuming loss control measures reduce losses by half, the effect is shown by line AC. The loss reduction costs, such as security and sprinkler systems, have not been included in the calculation. To determine the final outcome these costs would have to be further deducted from net worth.

Insurance

Alternatively the company may decide only to purchase insurance to finance replacement of the assets subject to loss. The effect of this is reflected on the net worth as shown by line AD.

Loss control and insurance

If the company decides to implement both loss control measures and insurance, the position changes again. If we assume that insurance costs reflect the reduction in losses, they are halved. This may not be entirely realistic, but insurer discounts for certain loss reduction/control mechanisms can be substantial. The effect of this strategy on net worth over the period is traced by line AE in figure 1.2.

The figures and scenario in this example are hypothetical but they are illustrative of the contribution which effective risk management and risk financing can make to the growth or preservation of the value of the business enterprise or the ability of a public service organisation to provide continuity of service. It should also be noted that the contribution of loss control and risk financing is measurable in terms of net worth.

1.2.3 Relationship to Other Functions

Paper Clip portrays a number of issues in relation to the inter-relationships between the various functional areas in a modern organisation. To survive, the organisation has to meet these goals, and thus the general strategic management of the organisation is concerned with co-ordination of the research, production, marketing, distribution, personnel and financial functions to this end. From the Paper Clip example we can see that this can be severely limited by the incidence of pure risk events. Firstly, the impact of risk upon the ability of an organisation to fulfil its stated goals whatever these happen to be.

The overall goal of risk management is thus to minimise interruptions to the pursuit of organisational objectives through control of the frequency and severity of loss, and ensuring adequate financial provision upon the occurrence of loss to facilitate resumption of operations.

Secondly, as we have seen the outcome of the incidence of risk can be expressed in financial terms. In the example this was net worth but it could equally be some other indicator of financial performance such as earnings. In the modern business enterprise the goal of financial management is assumed to be the maximisation of the value of the organisation to its owners or shareholders. Losses thus reduce the return to shareholders.

Risk management's contribution to financial management is the protection afforded to the income stream generated by the organisation's assets. This is two-fold:

(i) through reduced need to replace assets; and

(ii) continuity of earnings because finance is available to replace assets subject to loss.

From the Paper Clip example we can see that it would be possible to measure the effectiveness of risk management techniques in financial terms. For instance the cost of risk reduction techniques can be compared to reduction in losses plus savings in premium costs. Although this form of analysis ignores the risky nature of the cash flows, risk management expenditures can be appraised on a basis common to the other uses of corporate funds and would thus have to satisfy the same criterion, namely to add value to the organisation. The final result may however have to be subject to qualifications relating to the nature of the exposure.

The risk financing programme has to be supportive of the risk management programme. It requires to be cost-effective but without jeopardising the primary object of funds being available when required. This involves a search for the least-cost method of finance subject to the criterion that funds be available as required. There has therefore to be a trade-off between savings and risk.

1.2.4 Risk Financing Objectives

Risk financing objectives have been divided into pre-loss and post-loss objectives. Pre-loss objectives are concerned with the operation and management of the risk management function. Post-loss objectives describe the condition of an organisation that its senior management consider minimally acceptable in the face of the most severe foreseeable losses.

1.2.4.1 Pre-Loss Objectives

The main pre-loss objectives are:

Operating efficiency

Or minimizing the costs of the finance subject to the constraint that funds have to be available at short notice. Finance is available from a variety of sources, each with their respective cost structures and degree of risk. For example, retaining the cost of the loss internally is more economic than transferring it to an insurer, but this has to be balanced against the additional administration and costs such as claims handling. Moreover there is an opportunity cost attached to the funds that have to be available in a liquid form to meet claims as they arise.

Acceptable levels of risk assumed

When a loss occurs the prime concern of general management will probably be that funds are available to meet it, not the cost of the funds. The risk manager has to demonstrate that sources of finance have been secured in respect of the various types and sizes of loss and that any risk retained is within the capability of the organisation to absorb. The level of risk and uncertainty assumed will vary according to the organisation. For example an organisation's desire may be for a 'quiet night's sleep' through what is generally regarded as the most secure source of finance – insurance – although this may be the least economical.

Conformity to legal restraints and provisions

The risk manager also has to ensure that the organisation abides by the various statutory provisions relating to the purchase of insurances. In addition there may be other contractual commitments that require the purchase of insurance that have to be honoured. The main implication of these provisions and commitments is the constraint that it places on the freedom of action in formulating the risk financing programme.

1.2.4.2 Post Loss Objectives

Generally these are minimum post-loss operating conditions defined in specific terms such as the maintenance of minimum levels of net worth, liquidity, earnings, continuity of operations or public image. The more demanding the post-loss objective, the greater the commitment of organisational resources that is required to finance it.

Survival

Survival as a post-loss objective is defined as the minimum resources required to:

- meet immediate financial commitments;
- provide a management structure;
- maintain public confidence in the ability of the organisation to produce its goods and services; and
- replace essential equipment to enable it to recommence trading following the loss.

The level determined by management can be expressed in terms of minimum acceptable levels of net tangible assets (net worth), working capital or earnings. The publicly quoted business enterprise also has to consider the effect of pure losses upon share price. The desire may therefore be to stabilise earnings through insurance.

Continuity of operation

Public service operations may have an obligation to maintain continuous operations, the implications of which are greater pre-loss commitment of resources to risk control and risk financing. Good citizenship may be important for many organisations which could involve commitments in excess of those required under the strict terms of the law.

These various goals have implications both for the extent of the finance that is required and the sources of that finance. The organisation may have to reconcile conflicting pressures imposed by these goals. The amount of funds that are required under the different goals vary and in some instances imply a substantial pre-loss commitment which could in turn be at variance with other objectives of the organisation.

1.2.4.3 Resolving Conflicting Goals

In the absence of a single court of appeal the organisation will have to balance the conflicting policies against each other when making a final decision. It may however be possible to settle some arguments by measuring the cash flows involved in each of the various options. For example: measurement of the balance of funds invested in loss reduction against the expected cash flow benefits of such a project; or evaluation of risk financing techniques in terms of the cash flows paid to secure the funds. The benefit of the preservation of public image in the wake of a large loss could also be estimated in terms of its effect on market share which in turn could be translated into earnings.

These varying cash flows occurring at different points over time can be reduced to a common denominator by means of the discounted cash flow technique (DCF), which will be explained in the next chapter. The result is the present value (PV) of the various cash flows whether these are inflows or outflows. The outflows for a project are offset against its inflows to produce the net present value (NPV).

Projects are then selected according to their NPV. Projects involving the investment or commitment of funds are ranked according to the size of the NPV, which must be positive. The larger the NPV the greater value added by the project. Where sources of finance are concerned the NPV will be negative. The organisation should thus select the source which minimizes the negative NPV.

1.3 RISK FINANCING VARIABLES

Contained within the risk financing decision there are certain key variables which determine the nature of the financing technique that will be used. These are:

- the features of the losses associated with the different exposures;
- the cash flows – their size, direction and time delay between inflows and outflows;
- the rate of return required by the organisation from its resources (both 'external measure' of return on capital employed ROCE and internal rate of return IRR or 'internal measure' where figures are discounted back to NPV).

1.3.1 Loss Experience

Loss experience has to be analysed to determine:

- the class of exposure;
- the frequency of occurrence;
- the severity of losses.

11

The results from this analysis can be used to derive the relevant cash flows to permit the evaluation of any risk control expenditure or risk financing techniques.

1.3.1.1 Class of Exposure

The importance of this variable is that different classes of exposure have different financing requirements due to the nature of asset subject to loss. Assets subject to direct loss from property and personnel risk are generally physical in nature whereas those subject to liability and pecuniary risk are financial.

In practical terms therefore the ease, availability and cost of replacement will vary according to whether the asset is a physical or a financial one. Furthermore, property exposures are likely to have a more immediate and less predictable financing need than liability exposures.

As physical assets are typically less interchangeable than financial assets, interdependency between operating units or machines can be an important factor in determining the scale of property risk. Replacement of the financial asset is generally more straightforward than a physical one. The extent of interdependency is thus important in fixing the level of interruption costs whether these be loss in profits, additional costs incurred or indirect costs.

The maximum value at risk is also a function of the class of exposure. It is necessary to ascertain this for individual exposures either to prevent underinsurance or ensure sufficient internal funds are available to meet a worst case scenario.

1.3.1.2 Frequency and Severity of Losses

Losses can be analysed according to the size and frequency of individual losses during a specified period, normally a year. The relationship between severity and frequency is represented in Figure 1.3 below, which reveals three loss layers classified according to frequency and severity.

The lowest layer represents losses which are small in size but frequent in occurrence. This pattern means that they are relatively predictable. Despite this predictability, there may still be a cause for concern as the total loss figure can represent significant loss of profit to the business.

The middle layer represents those which are less frequent in occurrence but greater in severity. The level of severity is defined as losses which will interrupt operations and place a strain on both cash flow and the ability of the business to meet its commitments.

Fig 1.3

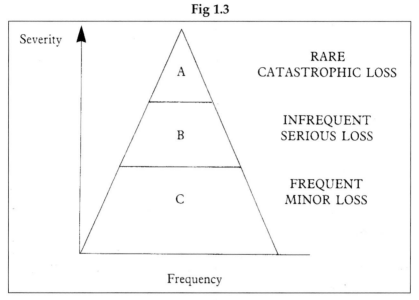

The Frequency and Severity of Losses

The upper layer is that of catastrophic loss. These are relatively rare occurrences but the severity is on such a scale that the viability of the enterprise is threatened. 'Catastrophic' has to be defined in terms of the scale of the organisation, but in any event the resources required to finance the loss are beyond its ability to provide from its own resources.

This method of analysing loss layers according to frequency and severity has been refined by B W Haines. This approach examines the frequency, probability and severity of likely events. A probability scale based on past experience is developed along the lines in Table 1.1. The probability refers to the chance of the event happening at least once during the period under review.

Table 1.1 – PROBABILITY SCALE

Factor	What the factor signifies
0	No loss is certain – loss is not possible
0.1	Possibility is very remote
0.2	Remotely possible
0.3	Slight chance of it happening
0.4	A little less than equal chance
0.5	Equal chance of it happening
0.6	Fairly possible
0.7	More than likely to happen
0.8	Predictable
0.9	Very probable it will happen
1.0	Loss is certain

Examples cited for a steel manufacturing plant range from 0.3 probability for fire or explosion arising from welding operations to 0.9 for petty theft.

Loss severity was graded on a range of 0 to 10. In the case of material damage it is appropriate to measure the monetary effects of loss or damage in terms of repair and/or replacements costs. Other considerations may apply for business interruption and legal liability exposures.

Table 1.2 – SEVERITY GRADING

Grading	Severity in general terms	Severity in money terms
0 1 }	Nuisance, current expense type	
2 3 }	Medium losses within the margin of the company's deductible (or excess)	
4 5 }	Manageable	
6	Range of largest previous losses	
7 8 }	Serious	
9	Most serious	
10	Catastrophic – total loss type	

The scale is determined by reference to the organisation's own resources. As a first step the mid-point of the scale (point 5) would be related to a level of loss below which the year's trading would not be adversely affected. It is recommended that this should be referred to the finance director or equivalent. Points 0 and 1 are then allocated to current expense type of loss and grade 10 to maximum possible loss. Note that for various reasons the maximum possible loss may still be less than the full sum insured value.

The final component of this approach – the frequency with which the events occur annually – is important because of:

(a) the cumulative effect upon a deductible, thus increasing the sum of the total monetary loss beyond the level of the deductible;

(b) the loss associated with trading pounds with the insurer for losses which are inevitable rather than insurable.

The purpose of these analyses is to provide guidance for risk financing strategy. The financing decision for each group of losses becomes apparent as outlined in Figure 1.4.

Fig 1.4

TYPE OF LOSS	FREQUENCY	SEVERITY	PREDICTABILITY	IMPACT	DECISION
TRIVIAL	VERY HIGH	VERY LOW	VERY HIGH	NEGLIGIBLE	NON INSURANCE
SMALL	HIGH	LOW	REASONABLE WITHIN 1 YEAR	INSIGNIFICANT	SELF INSURANCE
MEDIUM	LOW	MEDIUM	REASONABLE WITHIN 10 YEARS	SERIOUS	PART SELF INSURANCE, PART INSURANCE, PART TRANSFER
LARGE	RARE	HIGH	MINIMAL	CATASTROPHIC	INSURE

1.3.2 Cash Flows

The organisation also has to analyse its loss experience to discover the time period between occurrence and settlement of the loss, with a view to determining the pattern of cash flows for different exposures. The timing of the cash outflows created by losses is relevant to the calculation of present values and therefore evaluation of whichever source of finance is employed.

1.3.3 Time

Time is also an important element in a risk financing programme because of:

- the delay between incidence of losses and their settlement, as described above;

- the variability of losses over different time periods; and

- the constraint it places on the returns from retaining additional risk.

1.3.3.1 Variability

Time affects loss experience in the following ways:

- the longer the period, the greater the losses, i.e. losses vary directly with time;

- the longer time period also reduces the degree of risk or variability. The shorter the time period the more volatile the loss experience. This applies to both frequency and severity.

For example, if an organisation experiences an average of eight losses per annum, the probability that there will be a single loss during a year will be greater than during any quarter. Referring to the Poisson probability distribution, the probability that the organisation will have more than a certain number of losses during either of the periods is shown in Table 1.3.

Table 1.3 – PROBABILITY OF SUFFERING (r) OR MORE LOSSES IN EACH PERIOD

Number of Losses	Probabilities	
(r)	any one quarter	any one year
0 or more	1.0000	1.0000
1	0.8647	0.9997
2	0.5940	0.9970
3	0.3233	0.9862
4	0.1429	0.9576
8	0.0011	0.5470
10	0.0000	0.2834
16	0.0000	0.0082

The Probability of Organisational Losses

1.3.3.2 Constraint

By retaining risk an organisation enters into a trade-off between immediate savings in insurance premiums and the additional risk. A rough guide to the trade-off can be expressed as the number of years premium savings that would be required to pay for the additional risk should it materialise.

For example, if a £1,000,000 deductible yields a saving of £100,000; ten years savings would be required to pay for a loss of this amount. Management however may require a shorter time scale or payback period before it is prepared to accept the additional risk. Risk financing programmes have to take account of this constraint.

1.4 RISK FINANCING TECHNIQUES

Risk management practice normally divides risk financing techniques into the following categories:

(i) transfer to a non-insurer;

(ii) retention;

(iii) insurance;

(iv) alternative risk finance.

1.4.1 Transfer to a Non-Insurer

This is usually arranged as part of a contractual agreement transferring either the activity giving rise to the risk or the financial responsibility for losses arising out of the risk. These transfers are a common practice in some industries.

Transfers of financial responsibility in particular is a standard condition of contract in a wide range of business agreements such as those for the sale of goods, supply of services, carriage of goods and leasing or hire agreements. In some cases the organisation to which the risk is being transferred may not be aware of the liabilities that it is assuming under the conditions of the contract.

Contracts transferring a risky activity can be actively used in the management of risk by transferring responsibility to a party which is better equipped to manage and control the risk. In order to be effective both parties have to be aware of the condition and the transferee has to be financially compensated in respect of the additional risk assumed.

1.4.2 Retention

An organisation may decide to retain its losses as insurance may not be the most appropriate method of financing loss or it may not be possible or desirable to place some or all of a risk with an insurer. In certain circumstances it may be as cost-effective to retain potential loss as to place it with an insurer. This is especially true for losses on the lowest layer of the loss pyramid. Insurers usually recognise this point and are prepared to offer concessions in the form of premium discounts for the retention of some of the potential risk by the insured.

Other factors which would lead to retention include:

- exposures not legally possible to insure;

- exposures which are not insurable such as the hidden cost of losses; or

- exposures which are insurable but for which cover is either not available or is not available on terms acceptable to the insured.

The potential losses from an exposure can be retained either in whole or in part. They are retained in whole when the risk is uninsured. In this case the organisation is acting as its own insurer bearing full financial responsibility for the losses incurred.

Risks can be retained in part when the risk is insured. In this case the organisation contributes to the costs of the losses but under the terms of the contract this liability will be limited and the insurer will bear the remaining portion of the loss. Much retention of loss takes place in this way. The most popular device is the deductible under which the insured is responsible for the first part of each and every loss to a pre-determined level. Losses below this level are wholly funded by the insured while the balance of those in excess of it are borne by the insurer.

The motivation for retention will have a number of facets:

- there may be an economic advantage in retaining the funds that would otherwise be paid immediately to an insurer;
- the financial ability of the organisation to bear the risk;
- the loss characteristics of the exposure;
- the desire of the management to undertake the additional risk and administrative responsibilities.

For instance, losses from employer's liability exposure would probably be more acceptable than those from products liability.

Once the decision has been taken to assume the losses arising from an exposure whether insured or uninsured, the organisation has to decide how to finance the cost of retained losses. This decision may in part be dictated by the nature of the losses concerned. The options which the organisation has are:

- pay losses as they arise from cash flow;
- create an internal reserve fund to which funds are allocated in anticipation of the loss; and
- create an external cash reserve fund either in conjunction with an insurer or insurance intermediary, or as a separately incorporated insurance subsidiary.

1.4.3 Insurance

An insurer is a professional risk-bearer. In contrast to the third party assuming risk as one of the conditions of a contract, the transfer of risk is the main object of the insurance contract. Insurance is the transfer of the financial responsibility for the risk at the point of occurrence, and conventionally involves the insurer in a commitment to pay, although the terms of the contract have to be consulted as in some cases settlement by the insurer may be in kind rather than in cash.

As insurance is a contractual transfer of risk, the terms and conditions under which the risk is accepted by the insurer have to be scrutinised to ascertain the scope of cover. This is important when comparing competing covers or when purchasing cover in a foreign insurance market as the conditions of cover, limits of cover and definitions of exposures varies from country to country.

Provided the terms and conditions of the policy are met, payment of the premium secures a source of funds in the event of loss. The insured is thus exchanging the uncertain cost of retained losses for the certain and known cost of the premium. The costs arising from pure losses during the period of cover are then fixed for the insured. This stabilisation of loss costs means that earnings are less susceptible to the effects of pure loss than when these are retained.

Insurance however does not always fully compensate the insured for losses suffered. This may be the result of limitation of liability accepted by the insurer, poor management of insurances by the insured leading to gaps in cover or uninsurable losses. Some studies have indicated that sums paid by insurers in settlement of claims represent only about one eighth of the true cost of risk to the firm subject to the loss.

1.4.4 Alternative Risk Finance

Alternative Risk Financing (ARF) techniques have grown dramatically since the start of the 1990s. The trend amongst programmes that have been placed has been for a focused range of products and services, which are all designed to address significant risk issues within a variety of different industries.

These risk issues are not limited to the traditional fortuitous hazard risks but include issues ranging from the cost of capital in project finance to the capping of legacy liabilities for uninsurable risks in merger and acquisition activities. However, with the current hard market environment in 2002/3, inevitably alternative methods of financing risk for what may be considered to be traditional or conventional classes will remain topical.

ARF is predominantly a tool for the solution of larger issues. However, as any solution is designed as a specific response to a particular set of risk issues, there can be no universal definition of ARF or what constitutes a large risk issue. A more complete overview of ARF techniques is given in chapter 11.

1.4.5 Risk Financing Programmes

As indicated earlier in the chapter a risk financing programme will involve a mix of techniques. Use of these would be guided by the nature of the losses as depicted by the loss pyramid in section 1.3.1.2. Typical recommendations for risk financing techniques were presented in Figure 1.4.

The risk financing programme has to be constructed and reviewed in the light of the financial resources and activities of the organisation. Reviews will be necessary firstly to accommodate changes in operations and/or resources in the light of changing market conditions, and secondly as part of the normal monitoring process to ensure *inter alia* that:

- risks are adequately provided for whether by insurance or other means;
- overlapping or excess covers are eliminated;
- estimated maximum loss values (EMLs) and insured values are reasonable;
- reasonable levels of discount on deductibles.

2

ESTIMATION AND VALUATION OF CASH FLOWS

2.1 INTRODUCTION

In chapter 1 we noted that risk financing is concerned with the arrangements for funding of losses, whatever their cause. Fundamental to an informed risk financing decision is an intelligent appreciation of the underlying loss experience, the basic material of which is loss data.

This chapter will be concerned with interpretation and analysis of loss experience with a view to determining an organisation's risk financing needs. The discussion will presume a knowledge of the statistical analysis of risk and probability distributions. If you require to refresh your memory on these topics you should consult the relevant chapters from the IRM text, *Risk Analysis* by Prof Gordon Dickson.

2.2 SOURCES OF DATA

The main sources of data of an organisation's loss experience are:

- its own records;
- its insurers, although care has to be exercised when referring to insurers' data because:
  - it refers only to insured losses; and
  - there may be variations in classification of data between insurers.

As far as is practicable the collection of internal data should be conducted in a uniform manner throughout the organisation by such means as standardised pro formas for incident reporting.

The extent to which a risk manager wishes to rely upon actual internal data as the basis for predictions about future loss costs or probabilities of loss depends on a number of factors. These include:

- the number of loss exposure units from which the information has been derived;

- the period of time over which loss data has been collected; and

- the degree of diversification of the organisation, i.e. the number of physical locations at which the exposures are located and their geographical dispersion.

These factors determine the quantity of the data that is available for analysis and the degree to which it is sensitive to a loss in one particular location.

For example a small local car hire firm operating 10 vehicles is unlikely to have sufficient loss experience over the past year to permit a meaningful estimate of the probability of loss for the incoming period. If the small company has not incurred any loss does this mean that there is a zero probability of loss in the coming year? More years of experience would be required before that question could be answered, as in smaller samples the events which have occurred are given too much weight and those which have not are ignored. In contrast a national car hire company operating 2,500 vehicles will be able to estimate the probability of loss more accurately.

Furthermore a single plant with large exposures in terms of property and employee liabilities may incur a reasonable number of losses per annum, but internal experience may be inadequate to predict the incidence of large losses.

In addition to calculating objective probabilities, an organisation can draw upon subjective data. Subjective data draws upon the experience and expertise of practitioners in various fields to produce judgements concerning the probabilities of certain events and their outcome. They can be used either in conjunction with objective data or to complement the results from statistical inference.

Reference to external sources of information however may be desired or required to supplement internally generated information and for benchmark comparison.

These sources include:

- data shared with similar organisations;
- statistics pooled by industrial or employers associations;
- data collected by safety and loss prevention organisations; and
- statistics published by local or state and central or federal government agencies. Care again has to be exercised because of differences in classifications.

2.3 ADJUSTMENTS TO DATA

There are factors external to the organisation which will give rise to changes in loss experience and increase the difficulty in making exact comparisons of different years' experience. For instance recent increases in product liability and professional indemnity costs in Europe are attributed by commentators to be partly due to the trends of 'consumerism', a greater propensity to seek resolution of the matter by litigation and the increase in awards made by the Courts.

Raw data should be adjusted to take account of such changes to ensure, as far as is possible and practical, that like is compared with like. Inflation and changes in the scale of operation of an organisation can be adjusted as described below.

Changes in the technological, economic, fiscal, legislative, political and social environments are not so easily incorporated in such figures. Where these are important, such as in the case of a major piece of legislation, they should be noted as possible explanations for unexpected trends in the figures. The existence of such factors emphasises the need for caution when interpreting the results of analysis and reminds us of the continued need for judgement to be exercised by the risk manager.

The information in Table 2.1 is historical in nature, recording the actual cost of the losses in each of the years listed. The values in each of the years may not be directly comparable for a number of reasons. Inflation for example will distort monetary values. Changes in the size of the organisation will also have an effect on loss experience, as it would not be unexpected to find an increase in accident and damage claims if the motor fleet doubled from one year to the next.

Table 2.1 – AGGREGATE LOSS COSTS PER ANNUM
Motor Fleet Accidental Damage

Year	£'000
1	91
2	87
3	96
4	118
5	113
6	145
7	140

The Historical Recording of Actual Losses

2.3.1 Adjusting for Inflation

Monetary values can be adjusted by relating them to a common year, which serves as the base year. The monetary value of losses is then adjusted by applying a factor based on a price, cost or other index of monetary values which converts the values in other years to the value of the base year. The year chosen as the base can either be the current year or a year upon which the index of prices chosen has been constructed. The most widely known UK price index is the Retail Prices Index (RPI). A wide variety of other indices are published for the UK, and care should be taken to ensure that the choice of the index is appropriate to the circumstances. In the USA indices of claims costs have been developed by a number of organisations including *Best's Review* and the Factory Mutual Insurance group.

In the following example a hypothetical index is used to illustrate the process of adjustment, where the values are being adjusted to bring them up to current year values. The adjustment for each year is as follows:

$Lc = LRx \ (PIc \div PIx)$

where Lc   is the adjusted losses
       PIc   is price index for current year
       LRx is unadjusted loss figure for year x
       PIx   is price index for year x

To adjust the Yr1 value of losses to the base year of Yr7:

$Lc = £91,000(112/85) = £119,906$

You should try this for yourself for each of the subsequent years. The full results are given in Table 2.2. Note that the results have been rounded to the nearest £'000.

Table 2.2 – AGGREGATE LOSS COSTS PER ANNUM
Motor Fleet A & D

Year	Index	£'000 (Raw)	£'000 (Yr7 values)
Yr1	85	91	120
Yr2	94	87	104
Yr3	98	96	110
Yr4	102	118	130
Yr5	105	113	120
Yr6	108	145	150
Yr7	112	140	140

Adjusted Values for Each Subsequent Year

In this example Yr7 was chosen as the base year and all values were adjusted accordingly. Another year could have been chosen and the values expressed in those terms. If you are using a price index you will usually find that a year other than the current one will have been set equal to 100. In this case it may be simpler to relate the values to this year. Whichever year is chosen as base it is important to draw attention to the year in which the values are expressed as in Table 2.2.

2.3.2 Adjusting for Scale

As total losses are the product of the severity or size of each loss and the frequency with which losses occur, adjusting only for inflation does not take into account changes in the underlying number of units of exposure which may affect the frequency of occurrence. Changes in the scale of operations can be adjusted in a manner similar to the adjustment for inflation. This adjustment infers that the frequency of occurrence is known. Thus:

$Fc = FRx (Vc \div Vx)$

where Fc   is the adjusted frequency
      Vc   is number of vehicles
      FRx is the unadjusted frequency for year x
      Vx   is number of vehicles in year x

Care is required in the selection of the measurement of the underlying exposure (V). In the motor fleet example it may be a relatively simple matter of the total number of vehicles, but some other measure, such as number of miles travelled, may be preferred. This is a matter for individual judgment of the 'best' indicator of use and availability of data.

If the exposure under consideration is employees then the number of employees or the annual wages and salaries cost could be chosen. If a monetary value is to be chosen such as wage costs in employee liability, or turnover as in product liability, then the figures should be adjusted for inflation before adjusting for scale.

Table 2.3 – FREQUENCY OF ACCIDENTS
Motor Fleet Accidental Damage

Year	No of Vehicles	Frequency (unadjusted)	Frequency (adjusted Yr7 values)
Yr1	500	90	108
Yr2	500	110	132
Yr3	500	100	120
Yr4	600	100	100
Yr5	600	110	110
Yr6	600	130	130
Yr7	600	120	120

The application to our example

2.3.3 Loss Development Factors

The example we have been using has assumed that all losses occurring in each of the years have been settled, that is that all the losses incurred during the year have been paid by the end of the year. The figures would therefore provide a full and complete picture of losses arising from pure risk for the year. This is rarely the case as losses take varying lengths of time to be reported and settled. However the requirements of accounting practice often require that the organisation can only record a loss once a cash flow has occurred.

In practical terms, if an organisation wishes to record the total of losses arising from a single year, these delays will mean that annual adjustments to the losses paid figure will be required as outstanding claims are settled. The losses recorded figure for each year will therefore be a proportion of the final figure until all losses have been settled.

Thus, because of the distribution of the occurrence of losses throughout the year and varying settlement patterns of loss, at the end of a financial period the organisation's losses will take one of three forms:

(i) Settled: those that have been settled. The file on these losses is closed and their final cost known.

(ii) Reserved: those that have been partially settled. In this case there will be an outstanding reserve in respect of those which have not been settled. The file will be open and the final or ultimate cost will be unknown.

(iii) IBNR: those which have not yet come to light – the incurred but not reported losses (IBNRs). Both the incidence and cost of these losses is unknown.

Examples of these are shown in Table 2.4. Claims are numbered according to the year in which they were reported. In this example it is an historical extract from a claims record between 1997 and 1998. You will note that in some instances – 9800/1, 9900/1 and 9900/2 – the claim has been reported after the year in which it occurred. These are the IBNR losses.

Table 2.4

Year of Occurrence	Claim Number	Paid Claims	Reserves	Status
1997	9700/1	1,000	0,400	Open
1997	9700/2	1,000	0	Closed
1997	9700/3	869	3,700	Open
1997	9700/4	11,846	13,500	Open
1997	9800/1	0	2,500	Open
1997	9900/2	19,983	9,500	Open
1998	9800/2	15,000	0	Closed
1998	9800/3	1,200	0	Closed
1998	9800/4	1,000	0	Closed
1998	9800/5	890	0	Closed
1998	9800/6	0	4,000	Open
1998	9800/7	25,000	5,000	Open
1998	9800/8	0	5,000	Open
1998	9900/1	0	11,000	Open

An Historical Extract from a Claims Record Book

The organisation can draw upon its previous claims record to determine:

- the relationship between the losses settled by the end of a specified period – usually the organisation's financial year – and the final (ultimate) cost of these claims;

- the relationship between IBNRs and reported claims at the end of each financial year.

The implication for loss figures is that the data for the most recent years will show lower levels than for older years where the majority of the claims have been settled. This factor has to be incorporated in analysis of the figures. If from past experience a relatively constant pattern of claims settlements is discernible, the final cost will usually be a multiple of the sum of the claims paid in each of the preceding years. This multiple is often referred to as the Loss Development Factor (LDF). It will normally be highest for earliest years of experience and lowest for the oldest year.

Table 2.5 shows the position for motor third party liability. According to these records at the end of year t (the current period) only 40% of outstanding claims by value have been settled. As the period under review wears on this proportion increases until by year t + 4 all claims have been settled. This is reflected in the LDF.

Table 2.5 – MOTOR THIRD PARTY LIABILITY

Year	Claims Paid as Percent of Final Value	Loss Development Factor (LDF)
t	40%	2.50
t + 1	60%	1.67
t + 2	85%	1.18
t + 3	95%	1.05
t + 4	100%	1.00

The Position for Motor Third Party Liability

The probable final cost is then calculated by multiplying the loss figure for the year by the LDF for that year. Thus the final cost of losses occurring in year t is the cost of losses reported multiplied by the LDF. This can be applied to the reported losses in subsequent years arising from losses incurred in year t until all the claims are settled. The calculation is shown in Table 2.6.

Table 2.6 – MOTOR THIRD PARTY LIABILITY

Year	Claims Paid plus Reserves	LDF	Estimated Final Value
t	250,000	2.50	625,000
t + 1	350,000	1.67	584,500
t + 2	550,000	1.18	649,000
t + 3	580,000	1.05	609,000
t + 4	610,000	1.00	610,000

The Relation Between Reported Losses and Claims Settled

The initial estimate at the end of the year in which the losses were incurred based on the reported losses for the year was £625,000. This is revised as the years wear on and claims are settled in full. You will recall that these revisions are based on the previous loss experience. The actual final cost in year t + 4 is £610,000.

This analysis applies only to reported losses; the IBNRs have still to be estimated. Estimation of the number of IBNR cases is based on the relationship between IBNRs and reported losses gathered from observation of past experience. This is illustrated in Table 2.7 which also refers to the motor third party exposure.

Table 2.7 – MOTOR THIRD PARTY LIABILITY

Year	Number of Claims Reported	Final Number of Claims	Development Factor for IBNRs
t + 1	75	100	1.333
t + 2	85	100	1.176
t + 3	95	100	1.053
t + 4	100	100	1.000
t + 5	100	100	1.000

IBNR Cases and Reported Losses

To estimate the final value of the IBNR losses, the average final value of the reported losses is multiplied by the expected number of IBNR losses.

This figure is then added to those calculated from the reported losses to determine the estimated ultimate value of losses. Finally it should be noted that the derivation of the LDFs for reported and IBNR losses is not usually as straightforward as indicated in the above examples. This usually involves the use of actuarial techniques, description of which is beyond the scope of the text.

2.4 LOSS FORECASTING

Forecasting is based on the premise that the past can be used to predict the future. The methods discussed in this section represent different ways of discerning trends from the past that can be projected into the future. They are:

(i) rates of change;

(ii) time series analysis; and

(iii) probability distributions.

2.4.1 Rate of Change

This method measures the average rate of change over previous periods and forecasts a figure for the incoming year based on this rate of change. The data in Table 2.2 showing Yr1 – Yr7 losses adjusted for inflation is the basis of the following explanation. The rate of change is measured by calculating the percentage change from year to year as shown in Table 2.8.

Table 2.8

Year	£'000	Rate of increase (%)
1	100	
2	104	4
3	110	6
4	130	18
5	135	4
6	150	11
7	170	13

Calculating the Rate of Percentage Change

The average rate of change over the period is measured by the geometric mean. The geometric mean is said to be the nth root of the product of the n values. It is calculated in the following manner:

Geometric mean = $\sqrt[n]{x1.x2.x3...,xn}$

where x1...,.xn are the rates of change for each of the years
    n   is the number of years in the expression.

$$= \quad \sqrt[6]{4.6.18.4.11.13}$$

$$= \quad 7.92\%$$

which would imply that the loss figure for Yr8 (Yr7+1) would be:

$$£170,000 \times 1.0792 = £183,464$$

When all the movements are in the same direction, the negative sign indicating a decrease can be dropped and the formula applied as above. Hence, a constantly decreasing trend can be treated in the same way as a constantly increasing trend.

If there are changes of signs as a result of increases and decreases in the figures then an adjustment has to be made to permit the formula to be used. In this case increases would be added to 100 and decreases subtracted from 100 as illustrated in Table 2.9 below.

Table 2.9 – MOTOR ACCIDENTAL DAMAGE

Rate of change (%)	X-value
+10	110
+15	115
-10	90
+7	107
- 3	97
- 2	98
+5	105

Sign Change as a result of Increases and Decreases

Applying the formula:
Goemetric mean = $\sqrt[7]{110.115.90.107.97.98.105}$

$$= \quad 102.83$$

$$= \quad \text{an average rate of increase of } 2.83\% \text{ p.a.}$$

The geometric mean has limited applicability as its main use is to enable a forecast of the loss figure for the following year to be made. It does not indicate the extent of variation to be expected of the actual from the forecasted figure.

2.4.2 Time Series

Time series analysis is concerned with determining the relationship between a variable or variables causing change (independent variable) and those responding to the change (dependent variable) and expressing this mathematically. This expression can be used to predict the value of the dependent variable given changes in the independent variable. In time series the independent variable is always time. It is plotted on the X-axis.

Time series is concerned with determination of any trends in the data. The components of a trend are:

- long-term (secular) trend;

- seasonal variations in the secular trend;

- cyclical fluctuations arising from factors external to the data such as economic conditions;

- other factors such as political, social or legislative factors influencing the data.

In this section we will be concerned with deriving a secular trend since we are only dealing with annual loss information.

We will consider an application of the principles to the example from Table 2.1.

Firstly losses are plotted on a scattergraph to identify any secular trend. The result is shown below in Figure 2.1.

Fig 2.1

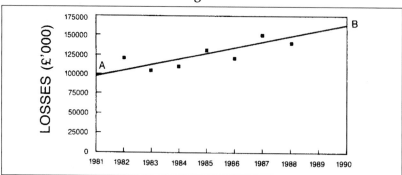

Losses Plotted to Identify any Secular Trend

The scattergraph reveals a direct relationship between time and the cost of losses. (Note that the points in the scattergraph represent only losses which have occurred, and therefore at this stage cannot give any information about the losses for the following year.)

The relationship in Figure 2.1 is therefore a simple one, the dependent variable being determined by a single independent variable. This may not always be the case as the behaviour of one variable may be subject to the behaviour of a number of others. Analysis of these relationships is beyond the scope of this text.

Determining the trend

To estimate the secular trend try to draw a line through the existing points which best 'fits' the points on the diagram, for example the line AB in Figure 2.1. The main problem with this approach is that more than one line could be drawn which could conceivably be the line of 'best fit'.

The figure for the next year would be determined by projecting the line into the future and reading off the value of the losses from the Y-axis. This method however lacks accuracy and is prone to the subjectivity of the person undertaking the analysis.

A more precise means of determining the 'line of best fit' is to use the least squares method which is based on the equation of a straight line:

$$y = a + bx$$

To discover the values for the constants 'a' and 'b', the steps are:

1. Convert the measurements of the X-axis from years, quarters or months into the number of time components in the series, with the mid-point in the series assuming the value 0. In the above example this would mean:

Yr1	Yr2	Yr3	Yr4	Yr5	Yr6	Yr7
-3	-2	-1	0	+1	+2	+3

NOTE

If there was an equal number of components then the years on either side of the mid point become -0.5 and +0.5, thus:

Yr1	Yr2	Yr3	Yr4	Yr5	Yr6	Yr7	Yr7+1
-3.5	-2.5	-1.5	-0.5	+0.5	+1.5	+2.5	+3.5

2. Add the values of y together.

3. Multiply each x-value by its corresponding y-value, and sum the products.

4. Calculate and sum the square of each x-value.

5. a = sum of y-values divided by the number years, months etc.

6. b = sum of x- and y-values divided by sum of x-squared values.

Using the figures from Table 2.1 we get the following results:

Table 2.10

YEAR	X	X^2	Y £'000	YX £'000
Yr1	-3	9	120	-360
Yr2	-2	4	105	-210
Yr3	-1	1	110	-110
Yr4	0	0	130	0
Yr5	1	1	120	120
Yr6	2	4	150	300
Yr7	3	9	140	420
Total		32	875	160

$$a = Y/n = 875,000/7 = 125,000$$
$$b = XY/X^2 = 160,000/32 = 5,000$$

Therefore if:

$$X = 3, y = 125,000 + (5,000 \times 3) = 140,000$$
$$X = -3, y = 125,000 + (5,000 \times -3) = 110,000$$

In reality, modern spreadsheet packages perform this calculation very quickly.

Forecasting

Once the equation of the line has been defined, the y-value can be forecasted by reference to the line.

It should be noted that applying the equation of the line to the x-values which have already been observed will not give the actual value for y, because the line that has been derived is the line of best fit, not the one which goes through all the points on the scattergraph.

As the expression only describes the relationship between observed data, care should be taken in drawing the line on the graph and interpreting the results.

When plotting the line from the equation, the 'a' constant denotes the Y-axis intercept. You will recall however that we have moved the point where x = 0 to the midpoint of the X-axis, which means that the value of 'a' according to the equation will be found where x = Yr4.

The equation of the line can then be used to project the line of best fit into the subsequent years. Thus:

$$y' = a + bx$$

Yr8 (Yr7+1) = 4, y′ = £125,000 + (£5,000 × 4) = £145,000; and

Yr9 (Yr7+2) = 5, y′ = £125,000 + (£5,000 × 5) = £150,000

These forecasts should be treated with caution as:

(i) they are based on historical experience;

(ii) they do not indicate whether the actual value will be above or below the line; and

(iii) they do not indicate the distance of the observed value from the line of best fit.

Trend analysis is concerned with situations where changes in one variable move with changes in another variable – in this case time – and is of use when the patterns of change occur in a predictable fashion. It looks for patterns in the movement of past losses over time and projects these patterns into the future in order to forecast loss experience. Probability analysis is used in a stable environment with a large volume of data on past losses to forecast probability of loss distributions.

2.4.3 Probability Analysis

Probabilities are used to express the likelihood with which an event can be expected to occur in a stable environment. For example, the probability of an employee incurring an injury, or of motor damage losses exceeding a specified threshold.

Probability values range from 0, meaning impossibility, to 1, meaning certainty. For instance a 0.5 probability would refer to a 1 in 2 chance of occurrence while a 0.01 or 1% probability would mean a 1 in 100 likelihood of occurrence. Probabilities can be derived in one of four ways:

(i) by reasoning – 'a priori';

(ii) where all possible outcomes are known;

(iii) through analysis of past data, such as the probability of theft from a dwelling house each year, in which case the requirement is that there be sufficient data available to carry out an analysis; or

(iv) where there is insufficient data or incomplete knowledge by reference to degrees of belief concerning the occurrence or outcome of an event – subjective probability.

Probabilities concerning loss experience are largely based on relative frequencies drawn from analysis of the recorded observations. On the occasions where there is insufficient data to perform such an analysis, the risk manager may be required to take account of subjective probabilities.

2.4.3.1 Annual Loss Severity

The relative frequencies of the distribution of the frequency of occurrence, the severity of loss or aggregate (total) losses can be analysed. Table 2.11 shows the frequency distribution of motor accidental losses based on the figures in Table 2.2. Relative frequency is equal to fx divided by the sum of fx for each class interval.

For example, £440,000 ÷ £850,000 = 0.571

Table 2.11 – MOTOR ACCIDENTAL DAMAGE
Annual Loss Costs

Loss £'000	f	x £'000	fx £'000	Relative Frequency
0 < 100	0	50.00	0	0
100 < 120	4	110.00	440.00	0.571
120 < 140	2	130.00	260.00	0.286
140 < 160	1	150.00	150.00	0.143
	7		850.00	1.000

The Frequency Distribution of Motor Accidental Losses

From this analysis we can see that in over 50% of the years recorded, losses fell between £101,000 and £120,000. If we assume that the conditions under which these losses were incurred are unchanged then relative frequency can be expressed as probability. Thus the probability that losses will be in the £100,000 to £120,000 range in the incoming year is 57.1%.

The expected value of annual loss (forecasted average annual loss) is calculated by multiplying the mid-points of the class intervals (x in the table) by the respective relative frequencies or probabilities as shown in Table 2.12.

Table 2.12

x £'000	Probability (p)	Cumulative Probability	px £'000
110.00	0.571	0.571	62.81
130.00	0.286	0.857	37.18
150.00	0.143	1.000	21.45
	1.000		121.44

The Expected Value of Annual Loss

The expected loss for the incoming year is £121,440. Since this is expressed in 1988 figures the projected figure for Yr8 (Yr7+1) will be this value inflated by the relevant index. If we assume an inflation rate of 7%, then the projected costs will be £121,440 times 1.07, which is £129,940. The cumulative probabilities also indicate a probability of 85.7% that losses for Yr8 (Yr7+2) will be less than £130,000 (Yr7 values). This information could be of use to the organisation when it is considering the retentions that it wishes to assume for the exposure.

2.4.3.2 *Severity Distribution of Losses*

Consider the information drawn from Tables 2.2 and 2.3 and shown in Table 2.13.

Table 2.13 – MOTOR ACCIDENTAL DAMAGE
Severity Distribution Yr1 - Yr7

Size of Loss	f	x	fx	Relative Frequency (p)	px
0 < 500	180.00	250	45000	0.3913	97.83
500 < 1000	134.00	750	100500	0.2913	218.48
1000 < 2000	86.00	1500	129000	0.1869	280.35
2000 < 4000	35.00	3000	105000	0.0757	227.10
4000 < 6000	14.00	5000	70000	0.0304	152.00
6000 < 8000	6.00	7000	42000	0.0132	92.40
8000 < 10000	4.00	9000	36000	0.0089	80.10
10000 < 12000	1.00	11000	11000	0.0023	25.30
	460.00		538500	1.0000	1173.56

Severity Distribution of Losses

where f is the frequency of occurrence
x is the mid-point of class interval
p is the probability

This distribution of the severity of loss may be useful to identify, inter alia:

- different loss layers;

- the number of losses within a specified range of severity;

- the probability of a loss being less or greater than a certain value or falling within a range of values.

These can be used to indicate risk financing needs and assist formulation of appropriate risk financing strategies.

Actual losses however are likely to differ from the expected figure. (If you look at Table 2.2 you will see that none of the actual losses are equal to the expected annual loss we calculated in Table 2.12.) In addition to the expected value therefore, the extent to which the losses are distributed or dispersed around the mean is also of importance, as it indicated the degree of risk which is measured by the variance or standard deviation of the distribution.

2.4.3.3 *Theoretical Distributions*

In Section 2.2 above we indicated that insufficient loss experience would lend bias to the data and may understate losses when the data is used for forecasting.

If limited data threatens to lead to bias in an organisation's frequency or severity distribution then it can refer to a theoretical distribution. Theoretical distributions can be expressed mathematically which makes it possible for the full range of occurrences and probabilities to be calculated.

For example the normal distribution, which can be used to represent the distribution of the aggregate cost of losses, is defined by means of the mean value and the standard deviation of the data available to the organisation.

Others include the negative exponential distribution, which can be used as a representation of the severity of losses; the binomial and poisson distributions, which can be used as representations of the frequency of occurrence. Reference should be made to internal or external assistance for guidance in their use.

In conclusion, caution has to be exercised to guard against the over-reliance upon the figures produced. They are based on assumptions which are rarely made explicit when the figures are produced. Figures also tend to lend a spurious accuracy to the analysis which may not be warranted. The need for the exercise of individual judgment still remains.

2.5 TIME VALUE OF MONEY

We have seen earlier that there will be a delay between the occurrence and settlement of a loss. In some classes of exposure this can be years rather than months and can be a relevant feature of an organisation's risk financing programme. This section introduces a technique used by financial managers to resolve the problem of evaluating cash flows that arise at different points in time.

The technique can be applied to appraisal of both loss prevention/reduction expenditure and risk financing techniques. The following discussion centres on the latter.

The length of time that elapses between a cash outflow (claim) and the subsequent inflows (premiums) is of importance because money has time value that derives from three factors:

(i) Delayed Consumption. An entity will require a return for delaying their immediate consumption, for example interest on cash investments.

(ii) Opportunity Cost. Since resources are finite, an entity will need to make decisions about consumption. The decision to consume today is at the opportunity cost of the interest earned in the future.

(iii) Inflation. In times of expected inflation, an entity will demand interest to ensure that the delayed consumption of today, can be fulfilled in the future.

2.5.1 Future Value

Given the rate of interest or return and the initial sum invested, the future value of the funds at the end of the year or for any number of time periods can be determined. For example the value of £10,000 in three years invested at a rate of 15% p.a. will be:

Principal			£10,000
Year 1	Interest at 15%	=	£ 1,500
			£11,500
Year 2	Interest at 15%	=	£ 1,725
			£13,225
Year 3	Interest at 15%	=	£ 1,984
Final Value			£15,209

The formula for this calculation is:

$$[FV = P (1 + r) t]$$

where FV is future value
P is the principal
r is the rate of interest
t is number of time periods

This could also be calculated by using financial tables from which the appropriate compounding factor would be selected and applied to the principal as follows:

1. select future values tables (see Table 2.14)

2. select relevant interest rate column (15%)

3. choose the period row corresponding to the number of time periods over which the investment is to be made (3 years)

4. multiply the principal by the value selected
   (1.5209 x 10,000 = 15,209)

Table 2.14 – FUTURE VALUE TABLES
Value of £1 invested at x% for n periods

Periods	8%	9%	10%	11%	12%	13%	14%	15%	16%
1	1.0800	1.0900	1.1000	1.1100	1.1200	1.1300	1.1400	1.1500	1.1600
2	1.1664	1.1881	1.2100	1.2321	1.2544	1.2769	1.2996	1.3225	1.3456
3	1.2597	1.2950	1,3310	1.3676	1.4049	1.4429	1.4815	1.5209	1.5609
4	1.3605	1.4116	1.4641	1.5181	1.5735	1.6305	1.6890	1.7490	1.8106
5	1.4693	1.5386	1.6105	1.6851	1.7623	1.8424	1.9254	2.0114	2.1003

2.5.2 Annuities

The future value of a series of cash flows of £10,000 per annum can also be calculated by reference to financial tables. Remember that a different compounding value will be required for each year's cash flows as there are different time periods involved.

Table 2.15

	£	Compounding factor	Final value £
Year 1	10,000	1.5209	15,209
Year 2	10,000	1.3225	13,225
Year 3	10,000	1.1500	11,500
Total			39,934

Different Compounding Values

If, as in this instance, all the cash flows are of the same magnitude, an even quicker method is available. A series of equal cash flows is an annuity for which financial tables have also been calculated. The annuity table is used in the same way as the other tables. The behaviour of the annuity means that annuity tables include the annuity for each period. Thus period 2 annuity factor is made up of:

– period 1 annuity plus the interest thereon plus period 2 annuity.

Annuity factors will always show year beginning values. To find year-end values:

1. go to the factor for the next year;

2. subtract 1.00 from the factor concerned.

In the example above this would mean:

1. refer to the factor for year 4, which is 4.9934;

2. subtract 1.00 = 3.9934;

3. multiply by £10,000 = £39,934, the same as calculating the future value by individual years.

Table 2.16 – FUTURE VALUE ANNUITY TABLES
Value of £1 per annum invested at x% for n periods

Periods	8%	9%	10%	11%	12%	13%	14%	15%	16%
1	1.000	1.000	1.000	1.000	1.000	1.000	1.000	1.000	1.000
2	2.080	2.090	2.100	2.110	2.120	2.130	2.140	2.150	2.160
3	3.246	3.278	3.310	3.342	3.374	3.407	3.440	3.473	3.506
4	4.506	4.573	4.641	4.710	4.779	4.850	4.921	4.993	5.066
5	5.867	5.985	6.105	6.228	6.353	6.480	6.610	6.742	6.877

2.5.3 Present Value

It is also possible to express values arising in the future in terms of their present values. This is of benefit to any organisation which has to take decisions concerning the commitment of funds in the present in the expectation of cash flows in the future. The sum of these present values can then be compared with the original investment to determine whether it should be undertaken. If the net present value (sum of present values less cost of investment) is positive, the project will be accepted.

Future cash flows are reduced to present values by rearranging the compounding formula:

$$PV = \frac{(Ct)}{(1 + r)t}$$

where PV is the present value of a future cash flow
    Ct is the cash flow in period t

Again it is possible to short-cut complicated arithmetic by use of the financial tables. On this occasion, the relevant table is that showing the present value of £1. We can illustrate its use by calculating the present value of a stream of cash inflows of £10,000 per annum over the next three years. Note that in this example the cash flows are assumed to arise at the end of the period. In this example we have used equal cash flows. It can also be used with unequal cash flows each year.

Table 2.17

	£	Discount Factor @ 15%	Present Value £
Year 1	10,000	0.8696	8,696
Year 2	10,000	0.7561	7,561
Year 3	10,000	0.6575	6,575
Total			22,832

Cashflows of £10,000 Per Annum

The present value of an annuity of £10,000 for three years can be calculated in the same way. The discount factor is 2.2832, making the present value £22,832. Note that annuities can only be employed when the cash flows in each year are identical.

This process is known as discounted cash flow (DCF) and is used widely by finance managers in the appraisal and evaluation of investment projects sources of finance.

The DCF technique can also be used when cash flows occur more frequently than annually.

To discount for a period of less than a year:

1. Determine the number of time periods over which the cash flows are to be discounted. For example:

    Length of time period   Number of time periods p.a.

    6 months   2
    4 months   3

quarterly		4
monthly		12

2. Divide the annual interest rate by the number of time periods. For example, if the annual rate is 12%:

Length of time period	Period interest rate
6 months	6% per 6 months
quarterly	3% per 3 months
monthly	1% per month

3. Using these periods and interest rates extract the appropriate discount factor from the present value tables.

The present value of four quarters' cash flows at a discount rate of 12% p.a. would be found by applying the discount factor for each of the time periods at 3% as shown in Table 2.18.

Table 2.18

	Cash Flow £	Discount Factor	Present Value £
March 31	10,000	0.971	9,710
June 30	20,000	0.943	18,860
Sept 30	15,000	0.915	13,725
Dec 31	7,000	0.888	6,216
	52,000		48,511

Four Quarter Cash Flow

3

NON-INSURANCE CONTRACTUAL TRANSFER

3.1 INTRODUCTION

The provisions of common law which have developed over the years dictate that:

- responsibility for losses of or damage to property is generally borne by the owners of the property. For example theft or damage to a retailer's stock has to be borne by the retailer itself; and

- responsibility for losses suffered by third parties is borne by the party whose activities have given rise to the loss. For example customers can sue manufacturers in respect of injury or loss attributable to faulty products.

Other chapters in this text describe a range of measures which organisations can employ to finance these losses. As it is possible under contract law to alter common or statutory law provisions relating to the apportionment of the burden of losses arising from pure risks by means of contract terms, this provides another means of financing risk.

The contractual transfers examined in this chapter are distinguishable from insurance because:

- the transfer of the exposure or financial burden of the loss is part of another business transaction and is incidental to the main contract;

- the third party accepting either the risks or financial responsibility for the risks is not an insurer in the sense that it does not seek to pool risks in the manner of an insurer;

- insurance is solely a risk financing arrangement. Non-insurance transfers can also be used to transfer risk exposures.

There is a large body of such transfers in everyday business use, many of which have not by convention fallen within the remit of the risk manager. Examples include those used in the construction industry, in the carriage of goods, by servicing departments in service or maintenance agreements, and in the leasing or hire of equipment.

However they also constitute potential areas of exposure as other organisations seek to transfer risks or the financial responsibility for the cost of risk upon the organisation by the same means. It is important therefore that sound principles be established for their use and management.

Typically the contract terms fall into one of two main areas:

(i) risk control transfers;

(ii) risk financing transfers.

3.1.1 Risk Control Transfers

Risk control transfers are transfers of the activity that creates the risk by requiring the transferee to perform some activity other than the payment of money. They require a commitment to act on the part of the transferee rather than to pay. Examples include leases, subcontracts and waivers.

Note that the risk control transfer only becomes effective upon the performance of the action ridding the transferee of the loss exposure, such as a subcontractor arriving on site to begin operations.

3.1.2   Risk Financing Transfers

Risk financing transfers are transfers of the financial loss arising from the occurrence of the risk. In contrast to risk control transfers, these involve a commitment on the part of the transferee to pay but not to act. Examples of these are indemnity agreements and hold harmless agreements.

3.2 CONTRACT TERMS

A contract will define the obligations of the transferee under the common law. The terms however may also be drawn in a such a way as modifies each party's responsibility under common or statutory law.

This can take the form of allocation of responsibility for joint fault or transfer of responsibility for all losses to the transferee except those which are the sole responsibility of the transferor.

3.2.1 Restating Current Law

In this case both parties restate their understanding of the legal position with respect to losses arising from material damage, business interruption, money and liability exposures in order to ensure that their intentions will be carried out. This is intended to eliminate or reduce the likelihood of:

- the contract terms being misunderstood by the courts; or
- the rights of either party being affected by future legislation or court judgements; or
- potential conflicts of laws arising as the result of losses suffered by parties from different jurisdictions.

These clarifications are incorporated by citing relevant provisions of the statute or case law, identifying the jurisdiction under which laws the parties agree to be bound, or giving an understanding of current law by means of a specific clause detailing the application of the law.

3.2.2 Allocating Responsibility for Joint Fault

In cases where fault has to be shared between the contracting parties, the common law rule is that liability is joint and that the apportionment of blame would be decided on the facts of the case. As this process involves the courts it can be time consuming and expensive.

This can be avoided if one party agrees to accept full liability for all claims arising from joint fault – thus specifically altering the usual application of common law – and holding the other party harmless. The transferor would normally be expected to compensate the transferee in the price of the contract for assuming the additional risk.

3.2.3 Transferor Liable Solely for Own Faults

With the agreement of the transferee the transferor can widen the scope of the liability transferred to include all claims incurred except those arising as the result of the sole fault of the transferor.

For example, a hold harmless provision would protect the transferor against all claims except those arising from its own fault, the terms of which could take the following form:

> "The Contractor shall indemnify and hold harmless the owner from and against all claims ... attributable to bodily injury ... unless caused by the Employer's act or omission."

Note that this clause only relates to liability for bodily injuries except those caused by the Employer.

3.2.4 Legal Constraints on Contractual Risk Transfers

It has been recognised by the courts and legislative bodies of many countries that where the parties to a contract did not have equal bargaining powers the stronger party could exercise this advantage to the detriment of the weaker party. This has manifested itself in harsh contractual terms and conditions, especially in the event of non-compliance or default. In the UK, as in other nations, a measure of protection has been extended to the party in the weaker bargaining position by both courts and legislature.

3.2.4.1 Common Law

The courts in the UK in the past have sought to redress imbalances in bargaining powers between parties and are guided by the following principles when deciding if the terms and conditions are to be binding on both parties:

- the contract in all other respects fulfils the requirements of a valid contract;
- the writing containing the contract must be a contractual document;
- reasonable notice of the terms must be given to the other party or parties;
- ambiguities in the terms of the transfer are to be interpreted in favour of the transferee;
- the terms of the transfer cannot be used to protect a third party;
- application of the doctrine of fundamental breach – i.e. the transfer will not be effective if the party relying on it fails to fulfil the basic requirements of the contract.

3.2.4.2 Legislation

The principal piece of UK legislation in this area is the Unfair Contract Terms Act (1977); although others such as the Sale of Goods Acts and the Consumer Credit Act 1974 also had similar intentions. The Unfair Contract Terms Act is of most relevance to the area of risk control and risk financing transfers because its provisions are concerned with the extent to which liability for injury or damage to third parties or their property can be transferred by means of contractual terms and notices.

Contracts (apart from insurance) which are subject to the Act are:

- contracts which create or transfer interests in land;

- contracts for the sale or supply of goods and services;

- contracts of employment; and

- contracts relating to the liability of occupiers of premises to persons entering them.

The Act affects the terms and conditions of exemption and exclusion clauses which seek to transfer risk and also the validity of disclaimer notices in garages, car parks, cloakrooms and so on.

Insofar as the terms of the Act impinge upon contractual risk transfers it deals with:

- the extent to which liability for negligence can be transferred; and

- the degree to which consumers can be made to indemnify the liabilities of others.

Liability for negligence

Section 2 of the Act provides that a person cannot exclude or restrict his liability for death or personal injury resulting from negligence by reference to contract terms or to a notice, whether this be a general notice for the attention of all or given to particular persons. Thus, under no circumstances can liability for death or personal injury be transferred. However liability for loss or damage to property can be transferred subject to the satisfaction of certain conditions.

The contract condition or notice given must satisfy the requirement of reasonableness. Reasonableness depends upon such factors as:

- the relative bargaining powers of the parties;

- whether any inducement has been used to get the transferee to accept liability;

- whether the transferee knew or ought reasonably to have known of the extent of the terms of the clause;

- whether it was reasonable to expect that it would be practical to comply with some condition which if not fulfilled would permit the exclusion or restriction of any relevant liability;

- whether the goods were manufactured, processed or adapted to the special order of the customer.

Indemnity clauses

Section 4 of the Act provides that a person dealing as a consumer cannot be made to indemnify another person in respect of liability that may be incurred by the other for negligence or breach of contract by reference to a contract term, except insofar as the contract terms satisfy the requirement of reasonableness.

Similar provisions can be found in the legislation of the USA. Given state and federal legislation there is a substantial amount of statutory provision in this area which varies from state to state. However, according to the American Insurance Institute in *Essentials of Risk Financing*, these statutes which apply principally to risk financing transfers can be classified as:

- those which prohibit transfer of a particular exposure;

- those which prohibit the use of particular wordings;

- those which prescribe the exact wording in any clause which the contracting parties choose to include in their agreement.

3.3 FORMS OF CONTRACTUAL TRANSFERS

We have already seen that contractual transfers of risk can be either risk control transfers or risk financing transfers. It is the intention in this section to examine some of the different forms which such transfers can take. The organisation can take advantage of the provisions of current common and statutory provisions or to alter these to protect its interest – subject to the constraints mentioned above.

3.3.1 Risk Control Transfers

These transfers involve a commitment by the transferee to act rather than to pay. They include leasehold agreements, subcontracting of specified activities, surety agreements, guarantees and waivers.

3.3.1.1 Leases

A leasehold interest in property is a right to property for a specified period which confers the right of usage to the lessee subject to certain restrictions, but does not, under common or statutory law, incur the obligations of ownership. Examples include lease of land, buildings and equipment and the hire of vehicles, plant and equipment.

A lease can be used as a contractual means of avoiding exposure to property damage and many of the other liabilities incurred by owners, except in those instances where the injury or damage caused to third parties has been solely due to the actions of the lessee.

The owner of the property can also protect his position by altering these provisions through contract terms. For example the hirer of a vehicle or the lessee of property can be required to return the property to the owner in the same condition at the end of the lease as at the beginning. The conditions may make exceptions for ordinary wear and tear or fire and flood to these requirements. The terms of the lease or the hire have to be consulted to determine the party responsible for loss arising from various sources and other expenditure that may be incurred during the period of the lease or hire.

3.3.1.2 Subcontracts

The appointment of subcontractors is usually made for reasons other than the transfer of risk, but it gives an organisation another opportunity to manage risk. They are appointed because of specialist skills and expertise in an area of activity unrelated to the main activities of the employing organisation.

Subcontracting thus allows the activity giving rise to the risk and the losses arising therefrom to be transferred to another party. The specialist knowledge of this party of the processes involved and their potential hazards should also promote the management of risk. This experience may be reflected in the subcontractor's insurance and other risk financing costs which would be lower than those of the appointing organisation.

Widespread use of subcontracting in some industries has led to the development of a standard set of terms and conditions in these industries.

The extent to which risk is transferred is often dependent upon the nature of the exposure concerned. Exposures to property, business interruption (or consequential) and personnel loss together with the responsibility for financing recovery from these losses are frequently transferred to the subcontractor.

Attempting to transfer loss in respect of claims from third parties may be more difficult as the third party may in the first instance seek to hold the transferor liable. The courts may support this view leaving the transferor to recover the loss from the subcontractor. Furthermore the court may hold that the transferor was partially responsible for the conditions that led to the injury or damage to the third party. Despite these problems this method is frequently used to shift exposures to organisations better able to prevent or to finance recovery from losses generated by particular activities.

3.3.1.3 Surety Agreements

A surety agreement is one where the risk that a party to a contract will not complete its part of the bargain, or behave in such a way as to invalidate the contract, is transferred to a professional risk bearer – the surety.

A surety agreement is a contract between three parties – the surety, the obligor and the obligee – in which the surety guarantees the performance, behaviour or completion of an act by the obligor (or the principal to a contract) to the obligee who has a contract with the principal. Thus the risk of non-performance or dishonesty is transferred to the surety. The suretyship is incidental to the main agreement between the obligor and the obligee.

Sureties bonds can take a number of different forms but fall into one of two types: those that guarantee performance as in a construction agreement; and those that guarantee the honesty or actions of a person such as an employee or the executor of a deceased person.

For example if a building contractor is employed to erect a building according to contract specifications there is a risk of failure to perform. This risk of default is transferable to a third party known as a surety.

The surety promises to provide the employer or principal with performance or failing that with indemnity for lack of performance. If the surety suffers any cost or loss from the contractor's failure to perform or indemnify then the surety has a legal claim against the contractor for recovery of such cost or loss.

As the suretyship is part of the contract the surety's liability is discharged upon completion of the contract, or some other event which affects the contract – such as the obligor releasing the surety from the contract or the contract being modified without the surety's consent.

3.3.1.4 Guarantees

A guarantee is similar to a surety agreement. The principal differences being that:

- the guarantee is a two party agreement;
- it is separate from the underlying contract; and
- the guarantor can only be called upon once all possible steps to make the obligor comply with the terms of the agreement have failed.

A point of importance arising from the separation of the guarantee from the underlying contract is that the guarantor may not be released from the agreement in the circumstances under which a surety would be. The position of the guarantor in these circumstances would have to be determined from the terms of the guarantee. Surety and guarantee agreements are complex, the drafting and interpretation of which should be referred to those with relevant expertise. "Properly used suretyship and guarantee contracts provide proper protection; misunderstood or misused they can become exposures to loss for all involved."

3.3.1.5 Waivers

Organisations can reduce or remove sources of risk by having parties with which they are contracting waiving or relinquishing their rights to sue in the event of a breach of contract or tort. The waiver will normally be contained in the original contract signed in advance of any breach of contract or injury or damage to the other party. To be enforceable it must be demonstrated that:

- the waiver was not obtained by coercion, fraud or concealment;

- it does not infringe statutory provisions; and

- it is undertaken subject to some financial consideration being made by the party protected by the waiver.

Although the waiver is a sound risk management tool it does not however apply to claims in tort arising from third parties which were not party to the contract.

3.3.2 Risk Financing Transfers

These transfers involve a commitment by the transferee to pay, the most common form of which is the insurance contract. Non-insurance forms of transfer are indemnity agreements and hold harmless agreements.

The indemnity agreement is an agreement to pay (or indemnify) the other party for losses it may suffer in carrying out the terms of the contract. It is a general term to cover any agreement relating to fortuitous loss to property, net income, services of personnel and liability claims. The provisions of indemnity clauses in contractual agreements are subject to the restrictions imposed by common and statutory law as discussed above.

A hold harmless agreement is a specific kind of indemnity agreement dealing with liability loss. Its terms require the transferee to hold the transferor harmless from specified classes of legal claims, either by providing the transferor with the funds to pay the claims and associated legal costs or to settle these costs itself.

As indemnity and hold harmless clauses are inserted as a matter of course in many contractual agreements, risk and other managers should recognise where to look for the more common varieties.

3.3.2.1 Construction Agreements

Construction activities give rise to many kinds of exposure. The key areas of risk are:

- damage to the principal's premises and other property whether this be owned or in his custody or control;

- bodily injury to persons;

- damage to the property of third parties;

- impairment of the environment;

- claims which are not dependent upon bodily injury or damage such as nuisance, interference with rights of way etc; and

- contravention of statutory regulations.

Liability exposures are of particular concern as these can arise not only as a result of the activities of the contractor but also those of subcontractors, of which in a large building or civil engineering project there may be a considerable number. The principal (owner/Employer) can seek protection against these losses by means of hold harmless agreements embodied in the main contract conditions.

In many countries standardised forms of such contracts have developed to cover all aspects of construction operations including the financing of pure risk exposures.

The contract terms relating to pure risk exposure will normally specify:

- the exposures from which the Employer or principal is to be indemnified by the contractor or subcontractors;

- the extent of liability;

- the obligations placed on the transferee with respect to the liabilities transferred, such as the requirement to purchase and provide insurance cover in respect of the exposure;

- the effect of bankruptcy of the Employer (transferor).

In the UK these provisions are contained in the standard form of building contract. The clauses dealing with liability losses specify that:

- liability for bodily injury rests with the contractor unless due to the negligence of the Employer;

- liability for damage to property rests with the contractor provided the Employer can prove the contractor's negligence; and

- that insurance cover be provided in respect of these exposures.

Notice that the terms of these clauses place burden of proof on different parties. Liability for injury is presumed to be the responsibility of the contractor unless the contractor can prove otherwise, whereas the burden of proof for damage to property is placed on the Employer or owner of the property. The terms therefore uphold the rule of common law but also provide the opportunity for this to be altered should the facts warrant it.

3.3.2.2 Sale and Supply Agreements

The risks involved in the sale and supply of goods are:

- damage to goods supplied;

- injury to persons or damage to property caused by the goods;

- infringement of copyright;

- replacement or recall of defective goods;

- return of goods unsuitable for purposes specified.

The burden of loss in the event of damage to goods supplied falls on the owner. This depends upon the point at which title to the goods is transferred which is subject to the terms of the contract and need not take place upon delivery of the goods to the purchaser.

For example:

- goods sold on consignment remain the property of the original supplier whilst in the hands of a distributor until sold to the consumer; or

- goods sold on hire purchase remain the property of the vendor until the final instalment has been paid.

The terms of the contract can be used to alter the common law position relating to the responsibilities of ownership, which can be divided and transferred at different times. A wide range of such terms have been sanctioned by the International Chamber of Commerce (ICC) – of which all major trading nations are members – for use in international trade.

The extent to which an organisation can modify its liability exposures depends upon the relevant contractual arrangements.

Producers may find themselves subject to liability claims arising out of defective materials obtained from suppliers which they have used in the manufacture of a product. Therefore a manufacturer purchasing materials can seek to incorporate a hold harmless agreement in its contracts with its suppliers in order to protect itself from such claims.

For instance a typical agreement will normally require the seller or supplier to hold the purchaser harmless in respect of claims arising out of a defective product, subject to some conditions and exclusions (loss arising from the purchaser's own negligence is usually excluded). The conditions and exclusions themselves are often a function of the relative strength of the bargaining positions of the parties.

If a seller is subject to such an agreement, it should ensure that similar provisions are contained in contracts with its suppliers.

On the other hand, purchasers may also be subject to terms in sales contracts which modify the liability of the seller. It is important to ensure that similar terms are used in contracts with their own customers.

For example the seller of agricultural fertilizer ordered a supply from a manufacturer. The contract included the following clause:

> "Every effort is made by the company to secure the highest possible standard of excellence of both materials and workmanship and every care is taken to make sure the product is perfect. Nevertheless all conditions and warranties whatsoever, whether statutory or otherwise, are hereby expressly excluded and it is the sole responsibility of customers to satisfy themselves as to the suitability for any particular purpose of goods manufactured, sold or supplied by the company."

The seller sold the goods without incorporating a similar clause into the contract. The fertilizer was found by a customer to be below standard quality and the seller was subject to a claim which could not be transferred to the suppliers with whom the fault lay.

3.3.2.3 Leasing Agreements

Leasing terms can also be employed in risk financing transfers to transfer the liability of the lessor to the lessee in respect of liability exposures arising out of the activities of the tenant, his partners, agents, employees, contractors, customers and invitees. For example:

> "Throughout the period of the lease the tenant (lessee) will keep the premises in good repair and condition ... and shall be responsible for any damage of whatsoever nature to the premises however caused during the period of the tenancy (lease) and shall repair to the satisfaction of the landlord (lessor) such damage ...

and shall fully and completely indemnify the landlord in respect of any claim for injury to any person or damage to property arising out of the use or occupancy of the premises by the tenant however such injury or damage shall be caused ..."

The terms of leasing agreements for plant, machinery, vehicles and other equipment are subject to the same risks for both lessor and lessee. In common with leasing of premises the terms of such contracts usually require that the property be returned to the lessor in its original condition subject to certain exceptions, such as ordinary wear and tear. These leases can also incorporate hold harmless clauses in respect of liability claims and may also have a requirement that insurance be maintained by the lessee in respect of the liability and other exposures.

3.3.2.4 Bailment Contracts

Bailment is said to be the temporary transfer of the custody of an item of property, normally in conjunction with the provision of a service relating to the bailed property, for which payment is made. It can appear in a number of guises, such as the provision of safe-keeping facilities, transportation services and where property is left for repair.

At common law the bailee is liable for losses caused by loss of or damage to the bailor's property, loss of profits arising from such loss, continuing expenses of the bailor incurred as a result of the loss, and other financial harm suffered by the bailor as a consequence of the damage to his property. The main exceptions to this are where the damage is attributable to ordinary wear and tear or an act of God.

The bailee can attempt to reduce, restrict or remove this common law liability by recourse to contract terms. In order for these terms to be enforceable the undernoted general conditions have to be met, namely that the exclusions:

- have been equitably negotiated;
- have been adequately disclosed;
- conform to trade custom and practice.

For example garage proprietors have sought to restrict or exclude their liability as bailees by posting notices on the premises and by suitable wordings on invoices and letter headings. The courts have held that notices posted on the premises are insufficient as the proprietor cannot prove that they have been read by the customers; however a clearly printed notice on a letter or invoice (called a disclaimer notice) may be effective.

The hauliers of goods by road, common carriers, are a specialised form of bailee. Contracts of carriage are regulated by standard contract condition as are the liabilities which the carrier assumes when accepting the contract to carry goods.

3.4 MANAGEMENT OF NON-INSURANCE CONTRACTUAL TRANSFERS

The main concerns with this form of risk financing are that:

- the contract terms may be unenforceable;
- the transferee may not have the ability to manage the risk;
- the transferee may not have the resources to finance it; or
- there may be a mis-match between the terms used with suppliers and customers leading to an unintentional assumption of risk or uncertainty regarding the responsibility for certain exposures.

It is important therefore in a programme of risk transfer by contract terms to ensure:

- consistency in the use and meaning of contract terms, for example whether the meaning of terms is to be defined by current law or by the organisation;
- feasibility through the use of conditions which other organisations are prepared to accept.

The organisation should aim to be aware of:

- the nature of the risk transfers which it has in place;
- the nature of the risk transfers to which it is subject;
- the scope and extent of the risks being transferred by the contract terms; and
- the direction of the transfer – that is whether risk is passed forward to the purchaser or backwards along the chain of supply to the supplier.

3.4.1 Factors Appropriate to the Use of Risk Transfers

Considerations relevant to the choice of contract terms and the manner of risk transfer are whether:

- the contract terms are enforceable;

- the transferee is able to manage the risk;

- the price paid or consideration made to the transferee in respect of the additional risk assumed.

3.4.1.1 Enforceability

Contract terms may not be upheld because:

- they are deemed to be unfair, whether under common or statutory law;

- they are in violation of public policy;

- the interpretation of the terms by the Court differs from that of the contracting parties;

- the terms under which a contract has been agreed are unclear.

For example goods offered on one set of conditions may be accepted by buyers on buyers' terms of business, which may be in conflict with the sellers' conditions. Unless it is made clear that the order is to be concluded on the sellers' terms the customers' terms of business will be treated as a counter offer which the seller accepts. The customers' terms of business will therefore be deemed to be those which prevail.

3.4.1.2 Ability to Manage Risk

In the case of risk control transfers it must be satisfied that the transferee has the expertise necessary to control the exposures and reduce the losses that arise. The transferee must also demonstrate that it has the necessary resources to fund losses as they arise, especially in the case of risk financing transfers. Where the risk financing exposures transferred are beyond the financial capabilities of the transferee, the purchase of insurance cover becomes a further condition of the contract.

It is also necessary to have regard for the implications for risk control of the contract terms. The transfer of risk may result in a separation of responsibility for incidents from authority for their control. For example in the event of the liability for negligence for the employees of the transferor, then the transferee becomes liable for their actions but has no control over their behaviour. There is also little incentive on the part of the transferor to control the activities of its employees now that financial responsibility for their negligent actions has been transferred to another party.

3.4.1.3 Adequate Consideration

In principle the transferee should receive sufficient benefit from the contract to cover the obligations that have been assumed. It may not however be possible for the transferor to offer the transferee reasonable consideration for the exposures so transferred in which case non-insurance transfer becomes a less effective mechanism for the handling of risk.

It is preferable that responsibility for losses and their control be in the hands of the same party. This requires that contract terms should clearly delineate the lines of responsibility from manufacturer through distributor to the consumer. Manufacturers therefore are made responsible for any defects in the product or misleading statements made by them concerning the product but not for the actions of the distributor in the storage of the goods or representations made by them to the consumer.

The following guidelines are fundamental to the proper use of non-insurance contractual transfers of risk. The organisation should:

- ensure that the transferee has the financial capacity to back up its commitment;
- require that a certificate of insurance for contractual liabilities be in place before contract operations begin;
- where necessary be named as an additional insured on the policy of the transferee;
- avoid undue severity in contract terms as this may prejudice their enforceability;
- avoid ambiguity. The courts will interpret the terms either according to common law or in favour of the weaker party, neither of which is intended by the transferor.

3.4.2 Control of Non-Insurance Contractual Transfers

To control the use of contract conditions it is necessary to develop a strategy:

- to identify circumstances under which non-insurance contractual transfers can be used effectively; and

- to ensure consistency in the treatment of the transfers used by the organisation or to which the organisation itself is subject.

Steps which a risk manager can take are:

(i) Alert staff dealing with contract terms in such areas as purchasing or sales; leasing of property and equipment; repairs, maintenance etc; to

   (a) the risks that exist;

   (b) the importance of checking contract conditions;

   (c) report any exclusion, hold harmless or indemnity clauses.

(ii) Alert staff engaged in the drafting of contract terms to the existence, possibilities and limitations of contractual risk transfer.

(iii) Educate relevant staff concerning the liabilities to which the organisation can be exposed through contract terms and give guidelines for their interpretation.

(iv) Institute a review of existing contract terms to identify agreements subject to standard terms and those specific to particular contracts.

(v) Analyse standard terms to identify and evaluate the extent of the exposure being accepted or transferred and determine appropriate treatment in conjunction with the corporate risk financing programme. This should become organisational policy to ensure consistency of treatment of these exposures.

(vi) Subject non-standard agreements to more careful and regular analysis.

Commercial realities dictate that it would be unlikely and unrealistic to expect an organisation to withdraw from negotiations over a prospective deal solely on the grounds of unfavourable exclusion, indemnity or hold harmless clauses.

In the event it is likely that the organisation will be faced either with not being able to transfer certain exposures or being subject to exposures that would not otherwise be assumed. The risk manager has therefore to explore other control measures such as modification of the contract terms to:

- remove 'unmanageable' exposures which are beyond the financial capabilities of the organisation to retain and/or which cannot be transferred;

- reduce the exposure that is assumed perhaps to bring it into line with the provisions of existing insurance cover;

- remove the existence of ambiguous language especially where problems of interpretation can be foreseen perhaps by the inclusion of definitions.

The extent of the exposure should be ascertained if possible and the decision taken as to whether any will be retained and to what extent. The availability of insurance cover for the risks assumed then has to be determined and the terms examined to ensure that they provide the necessary cover. Caution has to be exercised in this process so that exclusions to cover are carefully noted.

3.4.3 Principles for Non-Insurance Contractual Risk Transfer

The aim of the risk manager in the use of non-insurance contractual transfers is to allocate exposures to loss and the financial burdens of losses in such a way as to minimise the cost of risk both to the organisation and to society. The ideal conditions under which loss transference is practicable are:

- the transfer has been fairly bargained and the allocation of losses between transferors and transferees is clearly understood by all parties;

- the transfer agreement deals explicitly with all aspects of the loss exposure or of the actual losses;

- the agreement gives details as to how it is to be implemented;

- exposures and losses are transferred on a basis that is at least as economic as alternative reliable risk financing devices;

- transferees should be able and willing to meet their risk control and risk financing obligations promptly;

- transferees should have sufficient ability and authority to handle the risks for which they have been made responsible;

- the price or other legal consideration given by the transferor should make the transfer attractive to both parties.

4

SELF-INSURANCE (1)
PRE-CONDITIONS AND RATIONALE

4.1 INTRODUCTION

Recent developments in the insurance and reinsurance industry have promoted the use of self-insurance as a useful alternative to transferring risk. Self-insurance has become an important risk financing tool as a corollary of the development of risk management.

Self-insurance means that the cost of losses arising from the pure risks are borne directly by the organisation and not transferred to a third party. The result of this is that the organisation suffers a reduction in net worth through either a reduction in assets or an increase in liabilities as a direct result of the loss.

The term 'self-insurance' is subject to some debate because it is contradictory. Insurance by its very nature requires the participation of two separate parties in order that risk is transferred, and so if there is no transfer of risk – as is the position with all self-insurance plans – the term is potentially misleading.

A more accurate term is 'retention' as a means of describing the process. This term is preferred by the Insurance Institute of America. Nevertheless because of the widespread use of both terms in practice we will in most instances use them interchangeably.

Retention can be planned or unplanned as illustrated in Figure 4.1 below.

Fig 4.1

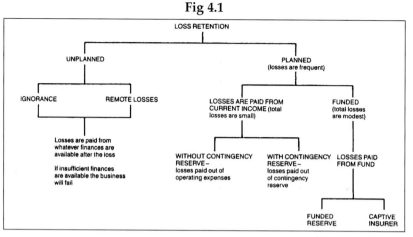

An Illustration of Planned or Unplanned Retention

4.1.1 Unplanned Retention

Risk managers seek to ensure that all retention of risk is planned but unplanned or unforeseen losses occur due to:

- exposures not detected until the loss occurred, as not all potential loss creating events can be identified;

- insurance cover not purchased;

- insufficient insurance cover as in the case of underinsurance;

- insurance cover unavailable;

- unsuccessful transfer of risk to a third party by reason of non-fulfilment of contract conditions;

- unwillingness or inability of a third party to which risk has been transferred to carry out its obligation, perhaps as the result of insolvency.

4.1.2 Planned Self-Insurance

An organisation will retain risks either because it chooses to do so or because they are unavoidable.

Self-insurance becomes necessary when:

- no insurance cover is available;

- the market is unwilling or unable to provide cover at least for the full amount of the exposure; or

- the risk is uninsurable.

There is already an element of self-insurance in most insurances as the financial compensation rarely fully covers the loss.

Planned or active retention of the cost of risk means that losses have been identified, measured and steps taken to provide for their payment when they arise. Self-insurance is undertaken where there is a sufficient range and spread of exposures and the benefits outweigh the costs. Growing use of self-insurance has led to the development of facilities and services to support this.

4.2 METHODS OF SELF-INSURANCE

Retained losses can be wholly self-funded or shared with an insurer in one of a number of ways, such as:

- excess or deductible;

- first loss cover;

- co-insurance; or

- retrospective plan.

4.2.1 Deductible

Under an excess or deductible arrangement the insured contributes a pre-arranged fixed amount to each and every loss in return for which the insurer charges a reduced premium. When the loss is below the deductible level the insured pays the full amount of the loss. For losses in excess of this the insured continues to meet the cost to the pre-arranged level with the insurer bearing the balance of the loss.

It is also possible to provide against accumulations of loss arising from either a single event under different lines of exposure or from a single exposure over a specified period by means of excess of loss and aggregate loss deductibles respectively. These were commonly available in the reinsurance market but in recent times the ability to secure this form of protection has diminished.

4.2.2 First Loss Cover

In effect, first loss cover reverses the operation of the deductible arrangement in that the insurer bears the first portion of the loss to a pre-determined fixed amount leaving the insured to finance the balance of the loss. The effect of first loss cover is to increase the dispersion of losses which the insured has to bear. In compensation the insurer charges a lower premium.

The arrangement is used in property insurances such as theft or sprinkler leakages where the likelihood of the loss of the full value at risk is thought to be remote.

4.2.3 Coinsurance

In this case the cost of each claim is shared with the insurer proportionately. This can occur through either an explicit arrangement between the parties or implicitly through the operation of the average conditions in property exposures when the sum insured is less than the value at risk. Under a coinsurance arrangement the insurer is responsible only for a percentage of each claim. The intention here is to secure a good alignment of interest between the insurer and the insured. In liability exposures the insurer may also place an upper limit on its liability leaving the insured with the balance of the exposure.

The premium charged will reflect the percentage of the risk financed by the insurer. The effect of coinsurance on the insured is to restrict the distribution of uninsured losses thus concentrating these within a smaller range. Moreover the dispersion of losses around the long-term average loss as measured by the standard deviation of the retained losses falls as the percentage of the risk insured increases.

4.2.4 Retrospective Rating

Under retrospective rating the organisation shares a portion of the total cost with the insurer in accordance with the insured's loss ratio. They are most commonly employed with liability exposures. The loss ratio can be based on either incurred or paid losses. The incurred loss retro is based on the losses which are expected to be incurred during the period of cover. Although there will be adjustments to the incurred loss figure the insurer retains the use of funds reserved for future losses. The paid loss retro is based on loss experience as claims are settled, and in this case the insured retains control of funds reserved against future losses.

A basic minimum premium is charged and a maximum premium is set, the actual premium being unknown until the end of the accounting period when the insured's losses become known. The higher the loss ratio during the previous period the higher the premium charged and vice versa. As with other loss sharing plans retrospective rating gives the buyer a reduced premium for assuming a portion of the period's losses. The amount which is saved however depends on the effectiveness of the insured's loss control measures.

4.3 CONDITIONS FOR EFFECTIVE SELF-INSURANCE

An organisation which desires to self-insure should be able to predict loss with reasonable confidence. A number of conditions have to be satisfied before a self-insurance programme for any class of exposure can be undertaken, namely:

- there must be a sufficiently large number of units of exposure;
- the company must have sufficient financial strength to absorb losses as they occur;
- management must be willing to undertake the necessary administration associated with a self-insurance programme.

4.3.1 Data

A sufficient number of exposures is necessary in order to generate the data necessary to permit the analysis of loss experience from which forecasts can be made. The data should be drawn from exposures which:

- are relatively similar in nature;
- have a small EML[1] in relation to the whole;
- are independent of each other; and
- are reasonably well geographically spread.

This dispersion reduces the overall level of risk as well as enhancing predictability.

---

1   EML = Expected Maximum Loss

Examples of such exposures include motor fleets, a chain of retail outlets, and school buildings within the jurisdiction of a local education authority. Thus a fire in one school is unlikely to spread to others, the breakage of plate glass windows in a single time period is likely to be a small proportion of the total, and it is unlikely that more than one vehicle in a fleet will be involved in an incident concerning others except where they are garaged overnight in the same location. It should be recognised however that there are perils such as storm damage, interruption to power supplies, terrorist or malicious damage which will affect a large percentage of the exposures.

4.3.2 Financial Strength

The organisation should have sufficient financial strength to bear the cost of losses, including interruption loss, as self-funding introduces an element of unpredictability. Retention requires that the organisation has sufficient financial capacity to meet these demands, particularly when loss experience is adverse. This can be funded:

- internally from cash flows or a reserve fund; or

- externally by borrowing.

4.3.2.1 Liquidity indicators

An organisation's tolerance to reduction in cash flow is determined by its working capital position. There are two generally accepted simple indicators of the working capital position, namely the current and 'quick' (or liquid) ratios.

The current ratio

$$\text{current ratio} = \frac{\text{current assets}}{\text{current liabilities}}$$

This is a measure of the ability of the organisation to meet its short-term commitments. It measures the ratio of current assets to current liabilities, the value of which is generally recommended to be 2:1, although this varies according to the industry concerned.

The quick (liquid) ratio

$$\text{quick ratio} = \frac{\text{current assets} - \text{stock}}{\text{current liabilities}}$$

This is also known as the acid test. It is a better measure of liquidity as stock, which can be illiquid, is excluded. The minimum recommended for this is 1:1 and indicates whether an organisation's immediate outstanding liabilities could be met from the assets which could be turned into cash quickly. The qualification with respect to variations across industries also applies to this ratio.

It would be expected that these figures would be above industry norms before retention is recommended. However, an organisation's access to contingent liquidity is also an important factor to consider.

Current and quick ratios are 'stock' concepts based on published balance sheet values. They suffer from the problems that they:

- only represent the circumstances of the organisation at one point in time; and

- are usually out of date.

Access to internal more up-to-date figures which the risk manager may have can help to ameliorate the latter problem but not the former. This can be overcome by referring to a Statement of Sources and Applications of Funds which shows the 'flow of funds' throughout the year by analysing the changes in assets and liabilities.

4.3.2.2 Borrowing Indicators

As we have mentioned it may be possible for the organisation to borrow in order to finance some of its losses. Prof R L Carter in *Risk Manager* (CII) lists three measures that could be used to determine an organisation's ability to borrow:

Ratio of liabilities to net worth

This is measured as below:

$$\frac{\text{total liabilities}}{\text{paid-up share capital and reserves}}$$

This gives the extent of total external finance in relation to shareholders funds, and consequentially the interest charges it will have to meet. This can affect ability to raise additional loan finance in the short or long term.

The capital gearing ratio

This is measured as below:

$$\frac{\text{fixed interest capital}}{\text{total capital}}$$

This ratio is similar in intent to the previous one in that it gives an indication of the ability of the organisation to attract external finance. It concentrates on long-term finance and is a measure of the riskiness of the position of shareholders and providers of loan capital.

Borrowing by a highly geared company is likely to be more expensive because of the greater risk to the lender. Shareholders will suffer an increase in risk also. This may be a constraint upon the risk financing strategy. The risk to the lender is highlighted in the final ratio.

The ratio of earnings to fixed interest charges

Referred to as 'times covered'. This indicates the extent to which earnings would have to fall before the interest payment to the lender would be threatened or 'uncovered'. In calculating this figure care is required to ensure that interest charges on prior loan capital, if any, have been included in the calculation.

As an example consider a company with the loan capital commitments shown in Table 4.1.

Table 4.1

	£	£
Earnings		100
Less: interest on loan stock		
10% Debenture 1995/96	10	
15% Medium-term bank loan	10	
12% Unsecured loan stock 1999	12	32
Earnings available to ordinary shareholders		68

Loan Capital Commitments

The priority of the distribution of the earnings can be depicted as shown in Table 4.2.

Table 4.2

Available earnings £	Net Income required £	Cum. total £	Per cent of earnings %	Cum. per cent %	Income cover
100	10	10	10	10	10.0
90	10	20	10	20	5.0
80	12	32	12	32	3.12

Priority of Distribution of Earnings

The bank loan is covered $100/(10 + 10) = 5$ times, and not 10 times because before the payment can be made the claims of the debenture holders must be met.

When using ratios it is inadvisable to rely on a single year's figures. At least three years' experience should be used; if possible it is worthwhile to refer to the same years over which loss data has been gathered.

4.3.2.3 Other Measures

Losses paid from either cash flow or a fund also affect earnings and net worth. The organisation has to decide at a senior level the variation in earnings and the reduction in earnings that it is prepared to accept. The levels set will affect the capacity for self-funding. **Earnings** are affected because revenue-generating assets (including those which are highly liquid) are damaged, destroyed or paid away, thereby depriving the organisation of their income. Reserving funds for the replacement of these assets incurs an opportunity cost which results in lower earnings.

Net worth is reduced as the balance sheet value of assets falls as a result of the non-replacement of the asset or the outflow of funds to replace it. Alternatively if funds are borrowed to finance replacement then liabilities are increased. The level of loss to be retained can also be determined by the variation in net worth which the organisation is willing to absorb.

Whilst tolerance to risk should be an absolute debate in financial terms the establishment of a risk tolerance threshold is often difficult. Different perceptions within a single organisation are frequent and the attitude of one official to financial tolerance can be quite different to another. The risk manager also needs to be careful when seeking direction on this point and may need to seek several opinions from different financial and operational functions within the group.

4.3.3 Institutional Constraints

Institutional factors include:

- insurance regulations;
- regulations controlling the flow of foreign exchange; and
- tax regulations.

These issues are discussed at more length in the next chapter.

4.3.4 Administration

The final condition that we mentioned was that the organisation must be willing to undertake the necessary administration. In brief this will include:

- record keeping;
- claims administration;
- loss adjusting;
- analysis of loss experience;
- collection of data relating to all incidents;
- investment of funds in the case of a funded reserve.

4.4 INCENTIVES FOR SELF-INSURANCE

Having established some preconditions for the adoption of a self-insurance programme we can now look at some of the reasons for undertaking it. These fall into two main categories – economic and managerial.

4.4.1 Economic Benefits

The sources of the economic benefits are:

- savings made on insurer's loadings for expenses, profits and reserves;
- savings arising from good loss experience; and
- investment income on retained premiums accruing to the organisation rather than to the insurer.

4.4.1.1 Loadings

Premiums charged by an insurer contain elements for the recovery of claims, expenses, contribution to reserves and profit. Risks retained therefore produce an immediate saving on these non-claims costs.

The savings are not inconsiderable. Diacon in *Economics* (CII) cites evidence which shows that for 1984 business, the expense ratio – i.e. commission plus management and other expenses to net written premium – varied from 20.9% to 43.6% according to class of business. Unpublished research into the performance of the top eleven UK incorporated insurers (by premium income) in the general market for the period 1970 – 1984 indicated that on average the expense ratio amounted to approximately 30% of net written premium income. However, recent indicators show that many insurers are looking to reduce expense ratios to more acceptable levels and one should not assume that the previously high ratios are still a feature in today's environment.

The most fruitful source of savings are those losses which occur regularly and predictably from year to year. Purchase of insurance cover for these levels of loss is uneconomic as the insurer and the insured are merely trading pounds or dollars, as the insurer pays out very closely to what has been predicted and charged out to the insured in the pure risk premium.

The insured receives no benefit in the form of reduction of uncertainty with the result that the transaction becomes a 'pound (dollar/euro) swapping' exercise between the two parties; except of course that for each pound paid the insured receives only a proportion in return.

An added problem for insurance buyers globally is the noticeable introduction of insurance premium taxes. Insurance premium tax (IPT) in the UK is a non-recoverable form of VAT. Its current rate is 5% although this frictional cost is a tax deductible expense. For every £ or $ of swapping that happens with insurers (including captives[2]) IPT results in additional cost.

Another contributory factor is the manner in which the premium is constructed. Loadings are built into the premium rate which is applied by the insurer to the values at risk. The result is that the monetary value of the loadings increases in line with increases in the sum insured

---

2   See chapters 7 & 8 which deal with Captive Insurance issues

or the underlying unit of exposure. However, the expenses of the insurer may not increase at the same rate or at all in some instances.

Against savings made must be balanced the loss of services from the insurer, the cost of which is normally incorporated in the premium. Insurers argue that expense loadings are necessary for the provision of the full range of ancillary services such as claims handling, loss adjustment, risk analysis and other administrative functions which historically have been 'bundled' with the basic insurance product. Going it alone means that the insured is deprived of the experience and expertise of the insurer's staff and the economies of scale that the insurer enjoys in the provision of these services. Often the value of senior management time is not considered but is a real opportunity cost issue associated with the successful management of a self-insurance programme.

The value placed by management on these services affects the self-insurance decision. However the possibility of securing these services from an insurer or another party on a fee basis should not be overlooked. Experience in the USA has indicated that as the practice of self-insurance develops these services become available from insurers, brokers and others. Thus if insurance is to be purchased the cost of the ancillary services should be estimated if possible and compared with the alternatives.

4.4.1.2 Loss Experience

The pooling or combination of risks by the insurer means that the pure risk element of the premium is based on the loss experience of all members of the insurance pool. Insurers are usually prepared to allow deductions from the premium for features of the risk concerned such as sprinklers, materials used in construction, the design of a building and so on, but the discount is based on the original premium rate and does not reflect the experience of the individual insured.

Under this arrangement an organisation with a good loss experience can effectively find itself subsidising another with a poor loss experience. Although acceptable in the short term, in the medium to long term the organisation concerned would be unprepared to tolerate the situation and opt out of the pool. It would then be free to seek to take advantage of its good record by assuming more of the risk itself.

A company adopting this strategy has to accept that there will be fluctuations in the pure loss experience and moreover that there will be bad years as well as good. The insulation and security of insurance is no longer available. The risk retention decision is a trade-off between savings and the additional uncertainty that goes with such a decision. Savings are possible for exposures with low severity and high frequency for little additional risk.

Further, when a corporate insured has moved towards self-insurance it is often difficult to reverse this strategy in future years irrespective of the prevailing market conditions.

For exposures which occur less frequently and with a higher potential severity, savings have to be balanced against the additional risk incurred. Before deciding upon such a trade-off the organisation requires to have access to data of satisfactory quality and quantity and be able to interpret the results of analysis of the data.

4.4.1.3 Opportunity Costs of Insurance

The purchase of insurance has an opportunity cost. Money paid to an insurer cannot subsequently be used by the organisation to generate income. Instead the income accrues to the insurer during the period between payment of the premium and the date of settlement.

This is more important for some classes of exposure than others. For instance, liability claims take a number of years to settle whereas motor accidental damage involves a far shorter period.

Prof D Houston has formalised the position in the undernoted formula:

$$I = P (1 + r)^t$$

where   I   is the cost of insurance
P   is the premium
r   is the rate of return on capital employed
t   is the time period (in years)

Thus for a company with a rate of return on capital employed of 20% p.a. the opportunity cost of £150,000 for property insurances for a period of 1 year is:

$$I = £150,000(1.20)^1 = £180,000$$

This example is a simplification because it considers only one year and would have to be adjusted for cover extending beyond that period. Furthermore it overstates the cost because it ignores tax which is important as the cost of insurance in most countries is a tax deductible expense.

Self-insurance however is not without opportunity costs, which arise from:

- the losses;

- the lower rate of return on the assets held in a reserve fund (if any) to meet losses; and

- the additional resources devoted to administration of the self-insurance programme.

The cost of retention has also been formalised by Houston:

$$R = [L + S + X] (1 + r)^{\,t} - X (1 + i)^{\,t}$$

where   L is the average losses
S is the administration and cost of ancillary services
X is the reserve fund
i is the rate of interest on financial assets held in reserve fund

Therefore $[L + S + X] (1 + r)^{\,t}$ is the revenue lost to the company as a result of self-insuring the losses. This is slightly reduced by the investment income on the reserve fund $X (1 + i)^{t}$. This expression assumes that all losses are paid at the beginning of the year which is unlikely. If the value of L is expressed in present value terms then the present value figure of average losses can be used in the calculation.

Prof R L Carter and N Doherty have illustrated this in the *Handbook of Risk Management* by assuming that losses are paid halfway through the year. The value of L (present value of average losses) can then be expressed as:

$$L / (1 + i)^{\,t/2}$$

in order to give the value of L at the beginning of the year. $L / (1 + i)^{\,t/2}$ recognises that if losses are paid halfway through the year then funds can be invested at the beginning of the period (at i% p.a.) to meet the losses as they are settled. As the time period is 6 months, the exponent is 1/2 or 0.5.

You will notice that the rate of return on the reserve fund (r) is distinguished from the return on capital employed (i). This is because the return from funds invested in financial assets (bank deposits, government stocks, fixed interest securities, etc) is less than from those invested in real or physical assets.

To illustrate, assume that the expected losses from the example above are £120,000 in total, although they are settled halfway through the year. The other variables are:

S = £30,000
r = 20% p.a.
i = 15% p.a.
X = 100% of expected losses (L). This ratio is set by management and reflects past experience and attitude to risk.

Using these values the cost of retention is:

$R = 1.2[£120,000/(1.15)^{0.5} + £30,000 + £120,000] - 1.15(120,000)$
   $= £314,280 - £138,000$
   $= £176,280$

Comparing the opportunity costs:

$$I - R = £180,000 - £176,280 = £3,720$$

shows that since insurance has the greater cost, retention will be preferred. In this example the interest rate set at 15% is obviously too high compared to the interest environment today. Any reduction in interest rate is obviously sensitive to the calculations. The application of a lower rate is likely to make the self-insurance option less attractive. However, the cost of insurance in a low interest rate environment is likely to be higher.

These results have to be treated with some caution as they are sensitive to:

- changes in the timing and amounts of losses;
- the attitude to risk of senior management which dictates the size of the reserve fund;
- costing of the ancillary services; and
- the divergence between the rates of return on financial and real assets.

Finally it should be again noted that no consideration has been given to the effects of taxation. The tax position of self-insured funds is complicated and varies from country to country. In general, self-insured losses are allowable against tax when they are incurred but contributions to a self-insured fund are not.

4.4.1.4 Insurer Requirements

From time to time insurers may insist as a condition of cover that an insured take certain loss control measures. If these require additional expense an insured could take the view that these requirements together with the cost of the premium are too expensive. The main point of contention in this area is likely to be the extent of the discount which the insurer is prepared to give once these measures are implemented.

4.4.2 Managerial Incentives

These include:

- increased flexibility in the handling of risk;
- retention of control over the funds that would otherwise be paid to the insurer;
- increased potential to extend control over losses;
- greater control over the quality of ancillary services.

4.4.2.1 Flexibility

Under self-insurance risks can be handled in the manner deemed most appropriate by the company rather than the insurer. The availability of insurance cover could be conditional upon certain actions of the insured, or cover that is not required may be incorporated within a policy as dictated by underwriting conventions whilst omitting certain risks on the same basis. The insured therefore pays for one thing and gets another. The result is that the organisation's risk financing arrangements are dictated by insurers rather than the needs with which it is faced. Freedom of action is limited and managements are faced with paying for cover which is not required whilst foregoing cover on other more crucial exposures.

Self-insurance presents the option of allowing management to tailor the risk financing programme to the needs of the organisation. Such a programme could and probably would include insurance but on terms and for the purposes decided by the organisation.

4.4.2.2 Management of Funds

Retaining control of funds that otherwise would be paid to an insurer, particularly in the case of long-tail business, is likely to prove attractive due to the potential of investment income underwriting profit.

Careful planning of liquidity and cash needs in relation to the claims settlement pattern for different exposures can enhance the benefits by retaining funds in their most productive use for the longest period advisable. Even if this sophistication of matching assets to claims pattern does not exist, the assets in the fund will yield investment income which otherwise would have been unavailable. It should however be incorporated in any financial evaluation of the contribution of the self-insurance programme.

The main problem of retaining risk is to ensure adequate liquidity to meet claims as they fall to be settled. This demands that the assets be set aside in a fund to meet all but the most immediate needs and that the fund is protected from other uses by the organisation. This pressure will be particularly severe during a period of cash flow shortage, especially if there is a substantial pool of liquidity within the fund.

Other problems relating to the accumulation of these assets whether or not in a separate fund are:

- the administration costs including that of staff to manage a fund;

- the effect of inflation on the value of the fund and thus its adequacy to finance settlement of claims at future price levels;

- the effect of exchange rate movements on the value of the assets in the fund where contributions to and payments from the fund are made in currencies different from that in which it is held.

4.4.2.3 Loss Control

Self-insurance is a more effective form of loss control than apportionment of group premium costs on the basis of the loss experience because:

- the premium rate for a class of risk is based on the loss experience of the pool and not directly related to an individual insured's loss experience;

- premiums are also subject to market forces;

- the delay between the loss and apportionment of premium based on loss experience;

- premium costs are regarded as a central administration cost beyond the control of units incurring the losses;

- self-insurance means that the effect of losses is borne directly and immediately by the organisation.

Self-insurance thus concentrates the attention of management because the resources of the organisation are more directly and obviously at stake.

With sufficient knowledge about the losses it is possible to incorporate them within the overall budgeting process. The benefits of incorporation of loss costs within the budgetary process are:

- the cost of losses is recognised;

- units responsible for loss are recognised, and are required to be accountable for their performance and bear directly at least a portion of the loss;

- greater attention is paid to safety, risk reduction and loss control;

- the benefits of risk management and loss control can be demonstrated;

- it helps secure co-operation for risk reduction and control initiative; and

- it enables activity to be directed towards the overall risk management goal.

Regular reporting is also a feature of the budgetary process. Actual performance is compared with budget to detect variances in order that the necessary remedial action can be taken or revisions made in the light of unforeseen circumstances. The frequency of reporting depends on management requirements and the nature of the business, but in the case of loss experience the maximum would be monthly and the minimum semi-annually.

4.4.2.4 Ancillary Services

Retaining risk means accepting responsibility for provision of services such as claims handling, loss adjustment, loss control, risk analyses and so on. These services can be provided in-house or obtained externally either from firms specialising in these areas or insurers who are prepared to do so on a fee basis. Any savings in premium from retaining additional risk have to be weighed against the cost of these services.

Additional control can be exercised for example in prompt payment of claims, which in some situations could have considerable public relations value, or stiffer resistance to unjustifiable claims.

Services provided by the organisation's own staff can be more effective because:

- the organisation's responsibility for loss funding is more evident;
- there is greater incentive to co-operate with risk control measures;
- in-depth knowledge of staff of the organisation's activities and exposures is likely to be greater than that of the representative of the insurer.

On the other hand, the organisation should not lose sight of an insurer's wider breadth of experience, expertise and objectivity and the benefits which it is able to derive from the economies of scale on its administration expenses.

4.5 FEASIBILITY STUDY

A self-insurance programme has to be tailored to individual circumstances and the requirements of the self-insured. A team led by the risk manager but staffed by members from other areas of the organisation should be set up to carry out a feasibility study. Brokers or consultants can also be consulted to provide the expertise lacked by the team as necessary.

It should be borne in mind that insurers are prepared to share risk with insureds in a number of ways. The first task is therefore to determine which exposures could be self-insured and secondly the limits to that self-insurance.

Thereafter the team's work will proceed as follows:

1. Describe operations under review.

   For example, carriage of goods, manufacture of silicon chips, retailing of consumer products, etc. This is a useful starting point and is often a means of defining the problem. Potential areas of exposure may also be identified.

2. Collect data from past experience.

    This would include data relating to the number and nature of incidents, claim costs, the underlying exposures such as sums insured, wages, etc. This should be available from both insurance claims documentation and insurers' records for insured losses. In the event of retained losses, reference will have to be made to internal records.

    A minimum of three years' experience, adjusted for inflation and changes in the underlying exposure units, is required in order to bring these to current values. Changes which are not amenable to incorporation in the data should be carefully noted.

3. Analyse the incidents.

    Data is analysed to determine frequency, severity, and total costs. The nature of an exposure and the size of the organisation will determine whether there will be sufficient data to produce statistically reliable information.

4. Estimate frequency, severity and aggregate costs of future losses.

    This would require that claims development factors are derived from claims settlement patterns in order that the present value of estimated losses can be calculated. Claims development factors can be determined by reference to external agencies such as brokers or actuaries.

5. Identify alternative methods of funding.

    This would involve considering the options of wholly insured or self-insured; or partial retention by means of deductibles, retros, coinsurance or some other method.

6. Cost each option identified.

    This should be the associated administrative costs. In the case of a combination of retention and insurance it is likely that a 'what if' analysis of the various combinations be carried out to determine the least cost combination.

7. Select the most cost effective method.

This is chosen subject to the organisation's financial position.

The programme has to be monitored regularly. It is important to realise that a self-insurance programme is not a short-term measure as the underwriting experience will fluctuate from year to year. These variations may require that the mix of techniques in the programme be adjusted – especially in the light of changes in the cost of commercial insurance due to changes in the insurance market cycle – but not its abandonment.

5

SELF-INSURANCE (2)
ORGANISATION AND FINANCE

5.1 INTRODUCTION

Adoption of a self-insurance programme begs consideration of a number of issues ranging from the financing of such arrangements to the organisation of the programme. Whether a fund should be developed, the amount of resources committed to it, how it is to be financed, sources of finance, the effect of retained losses on the value of the organisation, whether there is limit to the risk retained and so on are all questions that have to be addressed.

5.2 FINANCING OF SELF-INSURANCE

The principal arrangements by which self-insurance is financed are:

   (i) non-replacement;

   (ii) current expense;

   (iii) contingency reserve;

   (iv) internal risk funding;

   (v) external risk fund; and

   (vi) captive insurance company.

Borrowing is another option but is primarily available only to larger financially healthy organisations. Not all borrowing need be unplanned as it can also feature as part of the risk financing plan together with the methods listed above.

The first five of these options are examined in this chapter. Captives will be examined in subsequent chapters.

5.2.1 Non-replacement

In this case the firm absorbs the loss and does not replace the asset. This course of action would only be considered if:

- replacement was not necessary to maintain continuity of production or service; and

- the asset has been running at a loss. Non-replacement would increase profitability as the drain on cash outflow would be reduced by more than the fall in cash flow. The organisation's net worth in balance sheet terms would be reduced by the historical cost of the asset less depreciation.

5.2.2 Current Expense

Sometimes referred to as non-insurance, this approach charges losses arising from certain exposures as they occur as operating expenses against cash flow. The essential features are:

- a conscious decision not to insure the exposure;

- losses classified as operating expenses;

- costs can be charged against monthly and annual budgets.

Careful analysis of frequency and severity is necessary to provide a realistic foundation for such information and increase the accuracy of prediction.

It is most suited to the financing of losses with relatively high frequencies and low severities which constitute an unavoidable regular expense to a business. For example accidental damage to vehicles, minor property damage, theft, stock shrinkage, and minor employer's liability injuries.

As part of the budgeting process, loss levels throughout the firm can be monitored allowing performance against budget to be checked and variations examined to determine their cause. It thus provides a valuable risk control tool.

The main disadvantages are:

- the loss has an immediate and full effect on the accounts;

- funds may not be available when required due to adverse trading conditions, actual results being significantly greater than predicted or both;

- there remains some exposure to possible catastrophe.

5.2.3 Contingency Reserve

A contingency reserve is an accounting device to segregate a portion of the surplus arising from the trading operations each year which is equal to the expected value of retained losses during the period. Funds are not held specifically to meet these costs and can therefore be used elsewhere in the organisation until required.

This however is a weakness as the funds may be committed to a project and are not available to finance the loss. Its use is not common and is not popular with risk managers. Today there is a general convergence of accounting standards. International Accounting Standard 37 (IAS37) relates to the issue of making accounting provisions. The UK equivalent is FRS12. Basically the ability to create non-specific provisions is now limited/impossible and the use of contingency reserves is generally not permitted from an accounting perspective.

5.2.4 Internal Risk Fund

This is also referred to as a self-insurance or contingency fund. It is a separate fund maintained with the sole intention of providing liquidity to meet pure losses as they arise. It may be operated:

- on a year to year basis; or

- as a means to spread the cash management of losses over a number of years.

The first option operates by means of creating a fund out of operating expenses and charging losses against this fund. It is appropriate for smaller, more frequent losses. Benefits include:

- pooling of the organisation's risks;

- retention of a higher level of risk than would be possible for individual operating units, for example as a deductible on group insurances at a level greater than could be sustained by individual units;

- savings in premium.

The second option is designed to smooth the cost of losses by spreading these over more than a single accounting period. It caters for losses with low frequency and high severity, where severity is on the middle layer scale of losses in the severity/frequency triangle. The scheme is funded by contributions gathered from operating units and can be incorporated within the normal annual budgetary process.

Contributions in either case should reflect the exposure or loss experience of individual units or divisions. They can be calculated on the basis of:

- underlying exposure; or
- the expected annual loss experience for each class of exposure.

For example turnover can be used for products liability, wage roll for employer's liability, or sum insured in the case of property damage. This figure is then multiplied by a rate based on either the insurance market premium rate, past loss experience or a combination of both.

A major point of concern is that the fund will be exhausted by losses either before it has become fully operational or once it has been established because losses have been underestimated.

5.2.5 External Risk Fund

The external risk fund was previously structured in an attempt to provide a mechanism to overcome the tax deductibility problem of contributions to an internal fund. As such it may be suitable to organisations which do not want to set up a captive operation or are unable to do so because of the nature of its exposures or insufficient premium to justify such a step.

Contributions to the external fund are paid to an insurer which in effect offers a 'fronting' facility and accumulates the funds in the same manner as for an internal fund. The theory was that this would allow the contributions to be treated as premiums. However, today the accounting interpretation of any transaction like this requires transparency. The basic point is that the insured must recognise all assets and liabilities associated with such structures and in most cases the tax treatment will follow the accounting interpretation.

The distinction from conventional insurance is that the insurer will only settle losses to the extent of the liquidity in the fund. Finance for sums in excess of this amount have to be the subject of a separate agreement. External funding introduces the subject of alternative risk finance. This is dealt with in Chapter 11.

5.3 ORGANISATION AND OPERATION

5.3.1 Organisation

The self-insurance programme can be implemented at both group and operating unit or divisional levels. The goals of self-insurance at each of these levels will be different.

At group level self-insurance provides:

- an overview of the loss experience of the group;

- a large database;

- the statistical benefits of combining or pooling the experience of similar exposures;

- a reduction in the relative variability of losses level of risk;

- greater financial capacity than individual units to absorb loss;

- potential premium savings through greater assumption of risk enabling higher deductibles to be negotiated;

- greater buying power and negotiating strength than could be commanded by individual divisions or subsidiaries;

- the economic benefits of specialisation by virtue of the delegation of the function to an individual or small group of staff.

These features mean that management can plan the financing of such losses and evaluate alternative sources of finance.

At the level of units or operating divisions, the risk retained should be tailored to the unit's financial resources. The principal benefit at this level is to bring the financial impact of loss and implications of poor risk management to the attention of management without unduly compromising the financial position of the unit.

5.3.2 Contributions

It is the responsibility of the risk management department to ensure sufficient funds to meet the exposures have been retained. This can be accomplished by means of a central fund contributed to by operating units and collected through the normal accounting system, often in conjunction with contributions to group premium expenditure.

Contributions have to produce sufficient funds from the units to meet the total cost of claims incurred over a specified period such as an underwriting year. They should reflect the exposure or loss experience of each individual unit in relation to the overall exposure or loss experience of the group.

They can be calculated on the basis of either:

- a flat rate;
- the underlying exposure of the self-insured programme; or
- the expected annual loss experience.

For example turnover can be used for products liability, wage roll for employer's liability, or sum insured in the case of property damage. This figure is then multiplied by a rate based on either the insurance market premium rate, past loss experience or a combination of both.

Alternatively contributions can be based on average loss experience from previous years, adjusted for inflation rate and changes in the size of the exposure. This presumes that conditions in the next year will not change significantly from those in the years from which the average loss figure was calculated.

The individual operating units can also be protected against adverse loss experience giving rise to wide fluctuations in contribution level by means of limiting the size of changes from one year to the next.

A self-insurance programme allows the organisation to set the amount of the contributions, together with the timing and frequency of their collection. The benefits include:

- smoothing the risk financing costs of operating units;
- cross-subsidisation of loss costs where circumstances permit; and
- freedom to vary the timing of the collection of contributions to suit the cash flow of individual divisions.

5.3.3 Operation

Each year's contribution should be kept separate to allow for comparison of final settled costs with contributions, analysis of the timing of claims settlements and recognition of the value of investment income.

To institute the system the following are required:

- the maintenance of separate records for each underwriting year in respect of contributions, reserves against claims, settlement of claims and investment income;

- policies in respect of reserving for reported and incurred but not reported losses (IBNRs);

- arrangement for the management of funds.

5.3.3.1 Threats to Self-Insurance Fund

The main threats to an internal fund are:

- funds are siphoned off for use elsewhere in the organisation;

- inflation, especially in long tail business as claims are settled at price levels ruling at the time of settlement not those at the time when the contributions were received and the losses incurred;

- adverse loss experience which exhausts the fund; and

- potential for the operation of such a fund to be seen as an unlicensed insurance company operation.

Funds hijack

The chief measure against such action is to secure senior management understanding of the concept and commitment to the programme.

Inflation

The options available to counter the effects of inflation are limited. Of necessity funds have to be invested in liquid or financial assets which may or may not produce a real return – that is, above the rate of inflation. Negative real rates of return were experienced across a wide range of financial assets during the period from the mid 1970s to early 1980s. However subsequent experience has been that financial assets have been able to earn rates of return in excess of the rate of inflation. At the time of writing it would appear that this continues to be the case but the situation must be kept under review.

Exhaustion of the fund

A number of options are available to counter this problem:

(i) select classes of exposure with predictable loss experience. Avoid the more volatile and higher risk exposures such as product liability.

(ii) Do not include all exposures in the self-insurance programme in the early stages of its life. For example if an organisation had a property portfolio which was made up of 100 small retailing outlets and two large distribution warehouses, it would be advisable to split the exposure by retaining the risk in respect of the retail units and transfer the warehouse risk to the insurance market.

(iii) Contain or 'cap' the risk. Share it with an insurer by means of a per loss and/or aggregate deductible, retrospectively rated insurance or coinsurance.

(iv) Endow the fund by means of a capital investment at the beginning of its life. This can be for either whole or part of the amount required. Annual contributions would still be required from operating divisions.

Alternatively, a 'capital loading' could be included in the periodic contributions made by divisions over and above the amount normally required for annual expected losses in the early years of the fund. This would assist the rapid build up to a fully funded state. In conclusion it must be emphasised that since a self-insurance programme is a medium rather than short-term strategy any such programme has to be evaluated from that perspective.

Fund or unlicensed insurer

There are some concerns that the use of a structured fund dealing with separate parts of the same group could be seen as an insurer acting without an appropriate licence. Much depends on the legal entity status of the users. Risk managers should be encouraged to seek internal and (if necessary) external legal opinions on this issue.

5.3.4 Size of the Fund

The amount of funds to be held centrally is dictated by whether the arrangement is to be a central facility for the payment of losses as current expenses or an internal reserve fund.

5.3.4.1 *Current Expenses*

In the case of current expenses a large amount of liquidity is not required for the establishment of a fund for the losses concerned because:

- the losses are relatively stable and predictable;
- they are spread throughout the year; and
- each loss is rarely settled immediately.

5.3.4.2 *Internal Reserve Fund*

The position is different with an internal reserve fund because of the variability from year to year of the losses that it is used to pay. The fund has to be of a size which is sufficient to:

- absorb fluctuations in loss experience from year to year;
- ensure that it is not exhausted before it has been fully funded; and
- be balanced against the opportunity cost of the assets held in the fund.

Statistical constraints

The fund needs to be equal to:

- annual expected value of aggregate losses; plus
- a reserve to allow for fluctuations in loss experience.

The size of the reserve will be dependent on variations in loss experience. The degree of variation in expected losses is influenced by:

- the number of units of exposure;
- the degree of similarity of one to another;
- the extent to which loss of one will induce loss in another; and
- the number of different classes of exposure covered by the fund.

The degree of variation in outcomes can be measured by statistical techniques.

According to statistical theory, as the number and class of exposure units increases the degree of variation of losses from the average aggregate loss is reduced. Thus as the number and variety of exposure units covered is increased the requirement to maintain a proportionately larger reserve figure is reduced. It must be stressed however that whilst the degree of variability is reduced, the cost of losses in absolute terms will increase which in turn will require financing.

Management attitude to risk

This is generally assumed to be one of risk aversion. Some theorists have sought to construct mathematical models of risk profiles based on individual utility schedules but there remain serious conceptual and practical problems surrounding the measurement of risk aversion, such as:

- whose attitude has to be measured?

  - the risk manager taking the decision; or

  - the senior management team to whom the risk manager has to report who in turn are answerable to shareholders?

- the effect of group decision-making on risk attitudes has not been clearly determined.

- theoretical models assume that the attitude to risk is static. This is not the case as evidence suggests that it alters across time, probably, but not definitely, according to age and experience.

Some authors suggest a useful rule of thumb of an organisation's attitude to risk is its attitude to business or speculative risk. One which is prepared to take larger speculative risks is more likely to be prepared to retain larger amounts of pure risk.

This is often linked to the stage of development of an organisation. If an organisation is young, fast growing and dynamic then its attitude to risk is likely to be different from another which is a long-established, well-placed market leader with a stable management and market position.

These however are only pointers and each risk manager has to seek as best he can to identify the corporate attitude to risk-taking, particularly in the field of pure risk.

American authors Williams and Heins introduced the "worry value" concept as a means of quantifying the effect of the additional risk in monetary terms. 'Worry value' is based on the notion that since insurance transfers responsibility for financing the loss it provides a 'quiet night's sleep', it has a nil worry value.

Worry value increases with the level of retention and has to be incorporated into calculations for insure or retain decisions. The usefulness of the concept is restricted to the extent that it illustrates the effects of attitude to risk.

Financial constraint

The organisation is also constrained financially by its ability to make contributions from cash flow at a level sufficient to make a fund viable, or its capacity to set aside funds sufficient to meet the calls upon it in the early stages or a combination of both.

This area has been discussed in the previous chapter.

5.3.5 Tax Issues

Taxation issues relate to:

- investment income; and
- contributions to the fund.

The investment income generated by the assets held in the fund is deemed to be part of a company's income and thus subject to corporation tax.

The tax treatment of the appropriation of cash flow to a central fund varies from country to country.

In the UK the general principle is that only expenses incurred 'wholly and exclusively' in the course of business are deductible expenses and allowable against tax. Note that there are some bodies in the UK such as local authorities to whom such regulations do not apply.

Insurance premiums qualify as a deductible or allowable expense. Contributions to a central fund are less clear. They may be made in respect of either:

- an identifiable expense which has been incurred but as yet unsettled; or

- losses which are expected but as yet have not been incurred.

Those made in respect of an identifiable expense would be deemed as allowable against tax, but those in the latter category are not. This prohibition would appear to be due to contributions being regarded as an appropriation of after-tax profits rather than an expense.

For organisations subject to corporate taxes this places self-insurance funds at a disadvantage to insurance. Table 5.1 illustrates this point.

Table 5.1

	Company A £'000	Company B £'000
Profits	1,000	1,000
Less: insurance premiums	(100)	–
	900	1,000
Tax @ 30%	(270)	(300)
Contributions to self-insured fund	–	(100)
Available to ordinary shareholders	630	600

The Disadvantages of Self Insurance Funds to Insurance

Although contributions to the fund do not qualify as a tax deductible expense, tax relief is available when the asset is lost and funds are expended to replace it. Tax relief on the contributions therefore is effectively delayed (or accumulated) until settlement of the loss. However, if the fund is not used up as losses the residual profit would add to the bottom line thus boosting the available profit to shareholders.

Finally before leaving this general area, it should be noted that in most developed economies there is a wide range of grants available from central government and other international sources. Grant aid or subsidies can affect the cost of a replacement and should be included in any calculations. Expert assistance and advice is obviously required in this area.

5.3.6 Constraints

There are a number of other constraints which can restrict an organisation's use of self-insurance:

- compulsory insurances. The class of business deemed compulsory varies from nation to nation and in the USA from state to state. The degree of restriction depends on the terms of the legislation enacting the compulsory insurances;

- where insurance of specified assets may be a condition of contract. For example a debenture or mortgage loan stock agreement requiring that the assets which form the security be adequately insured;

- long-term agreements with insurers, in which contracts of three years or longer are undertaken in return for discount on premium;

- regulations controlling and restricting the flow of foreign exchange to and from a country, making it easier for units in these countries to remit contributions to the central fund.

5.4 RETENTION LEVELS

If an organisation is going to self-fund then it must consider the level of risk that it regards is acceptable to retain. This level is determined by a number of factors including corporate philosophy and goals, past experience, financial strength and the nature of exposures concerned. Retention levels should be established to identify at what point corporate objectives are affected.

The time element is important because the frequency and severity of loss varies inversely with the length of time period. The methods discussed below assume all losses within a year, but the inverse relationship with time should not be overlooked when considering a specific situation. The retention level is set by reference to:

- the post-loss goal(s) of the organisation;

- the characteristics of the organisation;

- the financial complexion of the organisation.

5.4.1 Goals

This sets the level of operation or performance that the organisation wishes to achieve immediately following the loss, and can be expressed in a number of ways including:

- service to customers;

- production levels;

- market share;

- liquidity;

- long term earnings performance;

- net worth.

The presumption is that in the event of a loss the amount of resources required to move from the post-loss to this desired position is known or can be determined. Given this information the appropriate financing arrangements can be made.

The features which determine the resources that an organisation has available to it following a loss, and which fix the financing requirements for achievement of post-loss goals are:

- the nature of the loss;

- whether property or pecuniary, personnel or liability;

- salvage and disposal costs;

- outstanding contractual commitments to suppliers, creditors and loan stock holders;

- income arising from activities in the pre-loss period; and

- trade credit and other arrangements that could be utilised or negotiated during the recovery period.

5.4.2 Characteristics of the Organisation

The level of risk to be retained is also a function of the nature of the organisation and its operations. Important factors in this respect are:

- the size of the organisation;

- the number of plants, operating divisions, subsidiaries, etc;

- the geographical location and dispersion of each plant or division;

- the maximum exposure at any single location;

- the degree of interdependency between plants;

- the contribution to profit from each plant;
- the maximum fluctuation in profit that could be caused by a loss.

5.4.3 The Financial Strength of the Organisation

The ability of an organisation to retain risk is ultimately constrained by its ability to absorb larger than expected cash outflows. Retention levels are therefore set by reference to 'acceptable' deviations in certain key financial variables such as net worth, earnings or liquidity. A number of rules have been suggested by various writers over the years.

5.4.3.1 1% of Earnings

This 'rule-of-thumb' value specifies an acceptable variation in earnings of one per cent of earnings. However earnings are not defined.

Its weaknesses are:

- it is based on a single year's figures which may or may not be typical;
- it ignores other factors of equal importance to the organisation's ability to finance risk; and
- as it is based on annual figures it gives no guidance for shorter term considerations.

5.4.3.2 1% of Earnings plus Premium Savings

In this case the additional resources from premium savings are acknowledged. However the danger is that these savings will be seen as another source of finance to fund other projects or reduce liabilities.

5.4.3.3 1% of Net Worth plus 1% of Average Earnings

An average earnings figure is used in order to remove distortions caused by a single year's performance. The average is based on the previous five years' earnings.

Inclusion of net worth gives an indication of the asset strength of the organisation and thus its ability to retain risk and withstand shocks. Ability to overcome adverse trading conditions or pure losses is often related to the absolute size of the organisation, as the scale of its operations and balance sheet values can influence both the availability and cost of external finance.

5.4.3.4 Multi-Variable Constraint

The method explained in this section draws upon a number of key financial variables to determine the retention level.

The objective is to determine the ability to finance losses in excess of 'normal' losses. Normal losses are defined as the average of annual losses for the previous three to five years. Note that given this information it is also possible to calculate the standard deviation of this loss distribution.

The models use the following indicators of financial ability:

    (i) financial strength;

    (ii) cash flow;

    (iii) earnings.

Financial strength

This is measured by:

- working capital: i.e. current assets less current liabilities;
- total assets: this is a measurement of scale which can be a factor in the ability to absorb or borrow to fund losses.

Cash flow

i.e. working capital less stock.

Earnings

This is made up of:

- earnings history, which is the average pre-tax figure from the previous five years;
- current earnings, which can be used to demonstrate the impact of the loss on a single accounting period. This is necessary as accounting convention dictates that losses be recorded for the time period in which they occur;

- sales, which indicate the ability of the organisation to generate revenue.

Once these values have been calculated they are weighted by means of applying a percentage to each one of them. The percentage chosen represents the amount of the variable that can acceptably be earmarked or reserved to fund losses. The percentage weighting is selected from a range according to Table 5.2 to reflect the business and financial conditions under which the organisation is operating.

Table 5.2

Component	Weight	Guideline
Working Capital	1 – 25%	Balance sheet inventory intensive, wide fluctuations – select lower weighting (1 – 9%)
Total assets	1 – 5%	Highly leveraged/geared – select a low weighting; liquid or unmortgaged assets can bear a high weighting.
Earnings history	1 – 3%	
Current earnings	10%	This should be set by financial management. It will be regarded as necessary for quoted companies which are dependent on the need to preserve stock values in the market.
Sales	0.5 – 2%	High gearing should tend towards low weighting. Higher weights will also apply in industries with higher than average profit margins.
Cash flow	5 – 12%	High weightings can be chosen if there is a history of steady earnings and reliable cash flow.

Percentage Weighting Reflecting the Business and Financial Conditions

The mean and standard deviation is calculated from annual aggregate loss data. If losses are normally distributed it is possible to calculate by reference to the distribution of annual aggregate losses the values lying within certain boundaries such as 95% or 99% of the distribution.

The risk manager can compare the values at either the 95% or 99% level to the financial information that has been generated as above and judge the level of retention in excess of normal loss costs that could be accepted.

Table 5.3

I	Forecasted Normal Loss		£2,500,000
II	Expected Variance from Normal Loss		
	– 95% Confidence Level		£1,250,000
III	Financial Ability (Weighted Figures)		
	A	Financial strength	
		1. Working capital	£1,500,000
		2. Total assets	£3,000,000
	B	Earnings indicators	
		1. Earnings history	£1,800,000
		2. Current earnings	£2,300,000
		3. Sales	£1,750,000
	C	Cash flow	£2,800,000

Determination of Annual Aggregate Loss Assumption

For the purposes of illustration we shall say after consideration of the data the level selected was £1.8m. This is based on the earnings history figure and satisfies both the working capital and current earnings requirement. The annual aggregate loss assumption is shown in Table 5.4.

Table 5.4

Forecasted Normal Loss	£2,500,000
Financial Ability to Assume Loss	£1,800,000
Annual Aggregate Loss Assumption	£3,300,000

The Annual Aggregate Loss Assumption

5.4.3.5 Computer Simulation

The benefit of computer simulation is that it allows a greater number of variables to be incorporated than is possible under the previous methods. The aim of simulation is simple: namely to examine the impact of projected aggregate losses at differing levels of loss probability upon key financial variables. Description of the construction of such a model is beyond the scope of this text.

Simulation makes it possible to replicate a number of 'years' of loss experience. The effects of loss experience upon various risk financing alternatives under varying insurance market conditions can then be simulated to produce:

- least cost retention levels for each level of loss; and

- the effect of the various risk financing techniques upon such key financial variables as:

    - liquidity ratios;

    - sales;

    - profit margin;

    - earnings;

    - net worth, etc.

Best and worst scenarios can be explored to determine the effect on these and other variables.

Output for a five year period could be generated to give financial statements at different loss levels for each of the years together with selected financial ratios for each of the loss levels and the least cost retention level for each level of loss.

5.5 SOURCES OF FINANCE

An organisation can draw upon a number of sources apart from insurance to finance replacement or repair of assets subject to loss or damage. These sources can be classified in a number of ways:

- short (up to three years but normally less than one year), medium (three to ten years), and long term (more than ten years); or

- internal and external to the organisation; or

- pre-loss and post-loss.

Pre-loss financing refers to funds secured in advance of the loss. The conditions and costs under which these funds are made available are known prior to the loss occurring. The most common example of this arrangement is insurance where payment of the premium usually precedes the loss.

Post-loss financing is the securement of funds after the loss. The costs of finance are borne by the organisation after the loss irrespective of the source of funds. It is likely that the terms, availability and the cost of the finance will not be known until after the financing is arranged. Post-loss financing need not be unplanned but rather it may be part of a financing strategy in which it is judged that the costs and uncertainties of seeking to secure the finance subsequent to a loss are preferable to incurring the risk premium entailed in the purchase of insurance.

5.5.1 Cash and Other Liquid Assets

An important source is the cash and other liquid assets available to an organisation. The availability is obviously dependent upon the cash flow and liquidity position of the organisation. Evidence from the UK and US indicates that financing investment or reinvestment out of internal funds is not a serious problem for firms earning returns in excess of their cost of capital.

5.5.2 Overdraft Arrangements

In the UK the existence of overdraft facilities provides organisations with a flexible post-loss source of additional finance.

Technically, bankers view overdrafts as short term self-liquidating loans repayable on demand and subject to annual review, but in practice they are often automatically renewed period by period and thus become quasi-permanent finance. The overdraft is a flexible and convenient form of finance that is available with a minimum of fuss and is a useful supplement to liquid assets for dealing with smaller more predictable types of loss.

As a point of note, secured overdraft facilities may stipulate insurance of security subjects as a condition of contract.

5.5.3 Term Loans

The main features of this form of finance are:

- available from banks and finance houses;
- medium term finance (two to seven or ten years);
- lending is tied to a particular project;
- generally repayable in fixed instalments;
- interest rates and terms are usually fixed at the outset, although larger sums may be subject to review.

Banks may in some circumstance be prepared to consider larger medium term finance projects. These are often available from merchant banks in any of the major currencies and are usually tailored to meet the specific requirements of the customer. Repayment can be scheduled to match the cash flow of the project.

This source may be attractive for finance of small to medium size losses given the scope for scheduling repayments to fit cash flow. However the negotiations have to be conducted in the aftermath of loss and the willingness of the lender may well depend on the ability of the borrower to meet the requirements of the security for the loan, such as security over the assets of the borrower and the maintenance of certain balance sheets ratios.

5.5.4 Line of Credit

Another source of post-loss finance available from banks is a line of credit. It is similar in purpose to an overdraft, namely a readily available source of finance, the limits of which have been agreed in advance.

A line of credit is:

- a commitment by a bank to lend a certain amount of funds on demand;
- a commitment fee is charged at the outset for holding open the line of credit.

A variation on this theme is the revolving credit agreement which is similar in operation to credit cards such as Visa and Access/MasterCard. The borrower is allocated a line of credit and is free to borrow up to but not beyond that amount at any time. As earlier borrowing is repaid more of the line of credit is available for future borrowing.

Lines of credit rarely will be large enough to finance major reinvestment following losses of a catastrophic nature. However it is useful for the smaller more regular losses and can be used profitably in conjunction with other forms of financing to cope with larger losses, as in the case of a deductible on an insurance policy which may be financed on the basis of a line of credit.

5.5.5 Contingency Loans

A contingency loan is essentially a dedicated line of credit. It is a pre-loss arrangement available in the event of some adverse contingency such as property damage or liability award.

If it is arranged in respect of events with low probabilities then larger amounts may be available for similar costs than under ordinary lines of credit. The terms would be negotiated in advance of the occurrence of the loss and would fix whether the rate of interest would be:

- related to the rates ruling at the time of the agreement; or

- related to the rates ruling at the time of the loss; or

- allowed to float over the terms of the loan.

In common with other lines of credit the securement or contingency fee is paid when the agreement is struck.

The benefits of contingency finance are:

- the limits and terms known in advance of the loss, which facilitates risk management planning;

- finance is available quickly after the loss thereby reducing the level of interruption loss; and

- it can be secured for larger amounts than may be required for other commercial uses.

The use of contingency arrangements is not unknown in financial markets but it is not a common practice. However, the ability to secure contingency finance from the insurance markets is a developing concept. Chapter 11 expands on this subject.

5.5.6 Long Term Finance

Long term finance refers to debt or loan stock and shares.

5.5.6.1 Long Term Debt

Long term debt carries the right to receive interest at fixed rate or floating rates. Rates are determined by reference to bank base or prime rates or money market rates. Holders have the right of redemption usually at the instance of the borrower between dates specified at the time of the issue.

Corporate debt can be secured or unsecured, the security normally being given over some or all of the assets of the enterprise. The terms and conditions of the loan are contained in the trust deed for the issue. It appoints trustees to safeguard the interests of the debenture holders. Insurance of the assets subject to the security is often one of the conditions of secured loan stock agreements.

5.5.6.2 Equity

Shares represent the owners' interest in an enterprise. There is no guarantee of dividend or repayment upon liquidation. Shares issued by listed companies are marketed in the UK through rights issues. The fixed costs of issue are relatively high, estimated at 4.5% of the sum raised, and the documentation requirements are substantial. Each issue also has to fit into a Stock Exchange 'timetable' which infers a significant lead-in time.

The time factor thus makes equity finance unsuited to a post-loss position requiring finance immediately to reduce damaging interruption loss.

In conclusion long term debt and equity issues are unsuitable for financing small or catastrophic losses, but may be employed for large but not catastrophic losses.

6

DEDUCTIBLES

6.1 INTRODUCTION

Deductibles are a means of sharing the cost of losses emanating from pure risk exposures between insured and insurer. To the insurer it is a method of reducing the cost of the settlement of a claim by transferring liability for a portion of the loss to the insured. To the insured it is a tool to providing a measure of control over losses from retained exposures.

In this chapter we shall examine the nature of the deductible, the range of deductibles in use, the benefits accruing from the use of deductibles and selection of appropriate levels of deductible.

Deductibles in various guises provide a convenient and accessible means of arranging a self-insurance programme. For many organisations full retention of losses may be neither advisable nor desirable as the level of retention is dependent on individual circumstances, such as the nature of the exposure and the resources of the organisation.

The use of a deductible offers the insured:

- cash flow benefits;
- cash flow protection.

6.1.1 Cash Flow Benefits

Under a deductible arrangement the insurer offers a discount on the full premium cost to the insured in return for its contribution to the cost of the loss. As we have seen elsewhere, it is in the insurer's interest to transfer losses at lower levels to the insured because of the disproportionate administrative costs associated with these losses.

The benefits to the insured are that it receives immediate savings and an increase in cash flow. As the terms of the majority of insurance contracts still require that premium is payable at the inception of the policy period, this means that savings on premium costs are immediately available. Savings arising at this point in time are valuable as you will recall that cash flows at the beginning of a period are weighted highest in present value terms.

6.1.2 Cash Flow Protection

The capacity to self-fund losses is constrained by liquidity and time. The shorter the time frame the lower is the tolerance for interruptions to cash flow. For example the extent of losses which an organisation can fund in a year is greater than that which it can fund in a month. The longer time period allows funds to be built up and also reduces the variability of loss experience that is encountered on a monthly basis.

The use of a deductible places a ceiling on the amount that the organisation has to contribute to each loss when it is settled. This reduces the risk of disruption to cash flow, or premature exhaustion of a fund if one exists, and allows the organisation to contain its liability for pure risk losses.

If a deductible operates on an 'each and every' basis this means that the total of retained losses assumed under the deductible can build up throughout the year. If a self-insurance fund were being operated this accumulation of losses could threaten its viability. These retentions arise as a result of the combination of losses (i) which are below the deductible level; and (ii) which exceed the deductible, in which case the organisation has to contribute the full amount of the deductible.

A second problem posed by the each and every deductible is that whilst it is effective in limiting the severity of loss it does not address the frequency of occurrence. For this reason an increase in the frequency of occurrence of losses in these circumstances is more serious than in the severity of loss – except of course where severity of loss is of a catastrophic nature.

This problem can be overcome by the use of an aggregate deductible, which although more common in reinsurance is also available in the direct market. For example consider the grouped distribution of losses for a year's experience in Table 6.1.

Table 6.1 – DISTRIBUTION OF LOSSES

LOSSES	FREQUENCY (f)	MID-POINT (x)	TOTAL (f) (x)
£		£	£
1 less than 5000	90	2500	225000
5000 less than 10000	6	7500	45000
10000 less than 15000	3	12500	37500
15000 less than 20000	1	17500	17500
	100		325000

If a £5,000 each and every deductible were to be applied the retained losses would be:

losses under the deductible	£225,000
losses greater than deductible (10 x 5,000)	£ 50,000
	£275,000

In this case the insured is paying for 87% of the total losses. This may be unacceptable for the insured who may want to stop the accumulation of losses for the year at £100,000. The insured may also be concerned that the frequency of occurrence in any one year is greater than the average figures in the distribution. For example if the number of losses increased by 10% across the board this would add a further £22,500 to costs below the deductible and £5,000 to losses greater than the deductible.

Aggregate or stop loss protection of £100,000 for the year could therefore be arranged in addition to a £5,000 each and every deductible. The insured's contribution to total losses is reduced to a maximum of 31%.

This example draws attention to the effect of a deductible, given a pattern of loss experience, on the manner in which losses are shared between the insurer and the insured. This in turn can lead to enquiries regarding the size of the premium discount that the insurer has been prepared to offer. These issues are, or should be, at the heart of any decision about the selection of a level of deductible.

Before we turn to examine a number of deductible selection methods it is worthwhile to stress that the results from any such methods, models or frameworks of analysis should be interpreted carefully.

Straightforward analysis and comparisons between, say, competing insurers or different levels of deductible are complicated by a number of factors such as competitive pressures for business, existing relationships with insurers, lack of sufficient loss data, variations between underwriters' discounts, solvency of insurers, variations in policy terms and conditions between competing covers, and interdependence of covers. Therefore there still remains the need for judgment based on expertise.

6.2 TYPES OF DEDUCTIBLE

The concept of the deductible requires that the insured bears a portion of the losses arising from pure risk exposures. As we have seen this can refer to losses from a single event or over a specified period. Each arrangement has a different effect on the distribution of losses that are retained by the organisation. The main forms of deductible are outlined in Table 6.2.

Table 6.2

EACH AND EVERY/PER LOSS	Otherwise known as the simple deductible, it is a deduction by the insurer from each claim settlement.
FRANCHISE/DISAPPEARING	Arranged on a per loss basis, the insured bears all losses up to level of deductible with insurer assuming the whole of the loss for losses in excess of the deductible. Most commonly found in marine insurance.
AGGREGATE/STOP LOSS	The insurer deducts a fixed amount from the settlement of claims accumulated over a specified period. More common in reinsurance markets.

Types of Deductible

The effects of each and every and aggregate deductibles were explained and illustrated by Professors Carter and Doherty in the *Handbook of Risk Management* as in Figure 6.1.

Fig 6.1a   **Fig 6.1b**

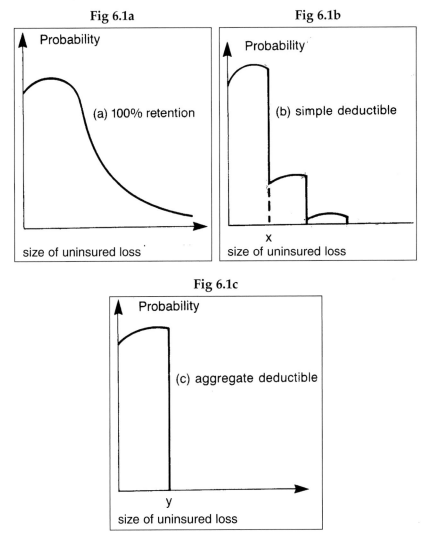

Fig 6.1c

Figure 6.1a illustrates the outcome if losses are wholly retained by the organisation and is included as a means of comparing the effect of the introduction of a per loss deductible or aggregate deductible on the distribution of losses. In Figure 6.1b the effect of introducing a per loss deductible is depicted. Notice that the range of losses is reduced but that the size of the uninsured loss is greater than the deductible for the reasons discussed in Section 6.1.2. This problem is overcome by the use of the aggregate deductible which confines uninsured losses within a predetermined range.

Deductibles are an effective method of reducing the dispersion of the probability distribution of losses. As you can observe the aggregate deductible is more efficient than the per loss deductible in this regard.

6.3 ANALYSIS OF THE SECTION OF DEDUCTIBLES

When an organisation assumes a certain level of deductible it means that it is engaging in a trade-off between premium savings and the additional level of risk. The decision according to Professor George Head of the Insurance Institute of America is bounded by the following parameters:

- the premium savings and costs associated with varying deductible levels;

- the financial capacity of the organisation to bear the loss;

- the degree of credibility or confidence that an organisation's management is prepared to assign to its own loss experience.

In models or methods of deductible selection most of the attention is focused on the first parameter. The degree of credibility is assumed in many models to be perfect – i.e. that actual losses will be as forecast. In practice the organisation has to accept that actual losses will rarely be as predicted.

The impact of the organisation's financial capacity on its ability to absorb losses can constrain choice of the deductible with the result that the organisation may be forced to select a less than optimal deductible level.

These three parameters are illustrated in the following analysis of the deductible selection decision for a per loss deductible by Professor Head.

The percentage premium reductions offered by an insurer when the insured assumes a deductible should typically increase at a decreasing rate. This situation is represented by the curve OP in Figure 6.2 which is the total premium savings for various levels of deductible, the slope of which becomes less steep as the curve increases in value. Experience in the market also bears this out, as insurers are usually prepared to offer more generous discounts for lower levels of deductible.

The total costs of assuming differing levels of deductible are represented by the curve CC. This shows that the cost per unit of self-insurance increases beyond a certain level of self-insurance. This arises because the organisation becomes less efficient the more it tries to behave like an insurer. If the opposite was actually the case then it should consider entering the insurance business!

There are fixed and variable costs associated with the deductible. Fixed costs, such as the cost of negotiations with the insurer, do not increase with the size of the deductible, meaning that the curve starts at OC and not at the origin. Variable costs are those which vary as the deductible increases. These would include:

- the cost of uninsured losses;

- administration costs;

- the net of tax arising from (a) reduction on tax deduction on insurance premium, (b) increased tax allowance for uninsured losses, (c) tax on investment income;

- opportunity cost of funds tied up in reserve fund (if any) to meet retained losses;

and would normally be expected to increase as the level of deductible increases but not necessarily at the same rate.

Fig 6.2

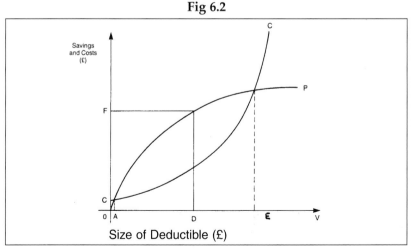

A Single Policy Period for a Property Exposure

The diagram in Figure 6.2 depicts the situation for a single policy period for a property exposure. The horizontal axis shows the value of deductible assumed ranging from zero at the origin to the full value of the property at V. The vertical axis shows the value of premium savings and the full costs of retaining losses under the deductible.

The area bounded by the two curves represents the net savings at different levels of deductible. Thus the organisation can derive net savings by the use of deductibles from OA to OE. In this analysis we are interested to determine the deductible level yielding the highest level of net savings – the maximising deductible.

In our diagram the maximising deductible is OD as this gives the greatest difference between the two curves. In geometric terms this occurs where the slopes of the curves are equal. In economic terms it means that the marginal saving in premium (MSP) is equal to the marginal retention cost (MRC).

The MSP is the additional savings in premium resulting from the assumption of an additional pound of deductible. The MRC is the additional retention costs arising from the assumption of an additional pound of deductible. When these are equal the point of maximum saving has been reached because to move from it would be to move to a position:

(a) where more savings could be made from assuming an additional pound of deductible (MSP>MRC), deductible level OF; or

(b) where the level of savings would be reduced (MSP<MRC), deductible level OG.

This conclusion is however subject to two constraints:

(i) the financial capacity of the organisation; and

(ii) the reliability or credibility of the forecasted retention costs.

The financial capacity will determine whether it is possible for the organisation to accept the maximising deductible. If it wishes to do so the financial capacity will have to be at least as great as the deductible multiplied by the expected number of losses during the policy period.

The financial capacity is defined as the limit of the organisation's ability to absorb loss retention costs from its own or borrowed funds while avoiding undue disruption of its normal activities. It can be measured in terms of earnings, liquidity and cash flow. The greater the ratio of earnings to the value of the property exposed the greater is the financial capacity to absorb losses. Likewise the greater the liquidity of the assets, the greater the loss retention capacity.

The effect of different financial capacities is illustrated in Figure 6.3. The diagram shows the position for two organisations of similar size and with similar property exposure, but with different financial capacities.

Fig 6.3

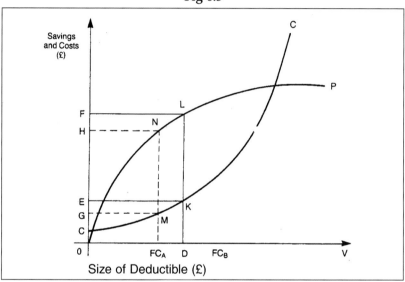

Different Financial Capacities for Two Organisations

FC$_A$ is the financial capacity of an organisation with low revenues in relation to property exposure and minimum levels of liquidity. FC$_B$ is the financial capacity of an organisation with a healthy liquid position and higher earnings to property exposure ratio. It is also likely that FC$_B$'s financial strength will give it access to additional external funds. Note that the use of ratios means that the principles can be applied equally to large and small organisations.

The effect is that Company B is able to select the maximising deductible, whereas Company A cannot and is forced to accept the deductible equal to its financial capacity. The savings are MN in contrast to KL enjoyed by Company B.

The final constraint is the credibility of the forecasted retention costs. In the previous diagrams we have assumed that loss retention costs as represented by CC were known. This is not the case. At the outset of the policy period loss retention costs are unknown and have to be forecast. Although these forecasts are based on past data it is unlikely that actual results will be exactly as predicted. This in fact is what has been assumed until now. To reflect this uncertainty various loss scenarios can be generated to simulate the effect favourable, unfavourable and expected results on loss retention costs. These are depicted in Figure 6.4 by CC_F which shows better than expected results and CC_U showing an unfavourable situation, with CC being the expected position.

Fig 6.4

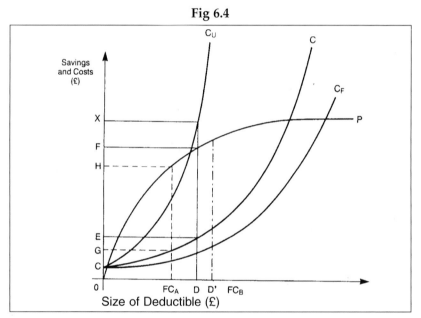

Favourable, Unfavourable and Expected Loss Retention Results

The effects on the deductible selection decision are relatively easy to trace. CCU reduces the savings from assumption of the deductible for both companies A and B. Company B in fact suffers a net loss PQ. On the other hand CCF enhances the position for both companies. And note that as the shape of the loss retention curve has changed so has the position of the maximising deductible, to OD1. An organisation can therefore be faced with either of these situations or a range of alternatives in between.

The key point is the degree of confidence that an organisation can place in forecasted loss figures. A number of statistical techniques can be used to indicate the reliance that an organisation could place on the predictions. The organisation however has to decide the level of uncertainty that it is prepared to accept.

From the foregoing discussions it would appear that the major constraint to the assumption of the maximising deductible is the financial capacity of the organisation. If this is raised or lowered according to the degree of certainty required, a measure of the tolerance for uncertainty would be to weight the financial capacity factor. Thus if an organisation was willing to accept a twenty per cent variation in result the financial capacity would be increased by this factor.

To recap, to select the optimising deductible (which is the maximising deductible subject to the above constraints), select the level of deductible which maximises the difference between premium savings and loss retention costs subject to the financial capacity of the organisation, adjusted to reflect the degree of risk acceptable to the organisation. Thus:

maximise $\qquad\qquad\qquad\qquad S - C$

subject to $\qquad\qquad\qquad\qquad D < FC (1 + R)$

where D   is the optimising deductible
      S   is the total premium savings
      C   is the predicted loss retention costs
    FC   is the financial capacity to absorb C
      R   is the acceptable degree of risk ($0<R<1$)

6.4 DEDUCTIBLE SELECTION RULES AND MODELS

The deductible selection rules or models discussed in the following sections are usually concerned with establishing the maximising deductible. The Houston model as modified by Greene and Serbein also has this aim but on the basis of its effect on the value of the organisation. Considerations of financial capacity and credibility are not explicitly incorporated and are left to individual judgment.

6.4.1 The Least Cost Rule

This rule was first suggested by Professor A. E. Hofflander and Professor L. L. Schkade. The rule is based on the proposition that the cost of pure risk to the organisation is equal to the insurance premium plus the cost of losses retained under the deductible. The initial formulation of the rule assumes that losses which occur under the deductible are equal to the full amount of the deductible.

The rule states that the level of deductible selected should be that which gives the lowest total expected cost (TEC). Formally, it is expressed:

$$TEC = P + qD$$

where P is the insurance premium
   D is the deductible level
   q is the average annual frequency of occurrence of loss for the exposure

To illustrate the rule in operation consider the following example of the accident and damage exposure for a commercial fleet of private cars. The premium information is contained in Table 6.3.

Table 6.3 – INSURANCE RATES (PER VEHICLE)
Commercial Fleet of Private Cars

Option	Premium (including IPT)	Deductible £
1	400.00	0
2	290.00	100
3	240.50	250
4	191.75	500
5	137.50	5,000
6	65.00	10,000

To judge the value of the deductibles some additional loss data is required. This shown in Table 6.4.

Table 6.4 – LOSS DATA FOR PRIVATE CARS
5 year period (Adjusted for changes in fleet and inflation)

Year	No. of Vehicles	No. of Incidents	Total Cost £
1	2000	320	82000
2	1700	200	70000
3	2100	480	110400
4	2200	640	163850
5	2000	360	87500
	10000	2000	513750

Analysis of this information reveals:

average number of incidents per annum	=	400
average annual cost	=	£102,750

To apply the TEC rule the value of q has to be calculated:

$$\frac{\text{total number of incidents}}{\text{total number of vehicles}}$$

$$q = 2000/10000 = 0.2$$

or

$$\frac{\text{annual average no of incidents}}{\text{annual average no of vehicles}}$$

$$q = 400/2000 = 0.2$$

We can now examine expected cost of the various deductible levels (Table 6.5).

Table 6.5

Option	Premium £	+	(q x Deductible) £	=	TEC £
1	400.00	0.2	–		400.00
2	290.00	0.2	100		310.00
3	240.50	0.2	250		290.50
4	191.75	0.2	500		291.50
5	137.50	0.2	5000		1137.50
6	65.00	0.2	10000		2065.00

According to the TEC rule, option 3 with the £250 deductible should be selected as it yields the lowest TEC.

This analysis could also be used to judge the reasonableness of the premium discounts for each of the deductibles as in theory the credits should reflect the expected value of the losses falling within the deductible.

For instance in the above example the deductible of £100 per car produces a premium discount of £110 (£400 – £290). The question is: is this reasonable in the light of the company's loss experience?

To answer this we need to identify the portion of the premium received that is used by the insurer to meet claims after expenses and other costs have been deducted. This is known as the pure risk premium. If we assume an expense ratio of 25% of gross premium the pure risk premium is £110 (1 – 0.25) = £82.50.

The insurer is thus charging £82.50 for £100 of cover. In other words this indicates that according to the insurer's figures 82.5% of all losses are less than £100. This provides a measure by which the insured can judge the premium discount.

If the company's experience indicates that losses less than £100 comprise less than 82.5% of the distribution of total losses, the company should self-insure because it is being charged more for these losses than they actually cost. Alternatively if the ratio of losses is equal to or greater than the 82.5% of this case the insurance cover should be purchased as the cost of insurance is less than or at least no greater than the actual cost of the losses.

The figures used are only illustrative but the principle can be applied at higher levels of deductible and more generally to other exposures. To confirm this we will examine the choice between options 3 and 4.

In this case the additional premium discount is £48.75. With the 25% expense loading this leaves a pure risk premium of £36.56. Since the additional risk is £250, this indicates that the insurer is charging £36.56 for £250 of cover: i.e. that 14.6% of losses fall between £250 and £500.

6.4.2 Paired Comparison

The paired comparison method suggested by Williams and Heins contrasts the additional benefits or savings with the additional risk from the higher level of deductible. This method concentrates on assessing the severity of loss. Its authors advocated it on the grounds that decision makers may find it easier to compare only two options at a time rather than consider simultaneously a whole range of possible options when making decisions. The method is a means of setting the choices open to the risk manager when selecting a deductible in order to highlight the differences between each of the options. It does not in the first instance require access to loss data or an analysis of loss experience although this information could prove a valuable help to the final decision.

We can illustrate this principle and its operation by referring to the example in Table 6.3 above. The first step is to arrange the premium schedule in ascending order of risk as in Table 6.3. Under the paired comparison approach option 1 is compared with option 2; option 2 with option 3; option 3 with option 4, and so on. The results of the analysis can be displayed to emphasize the difference between the first and the second options, the second and the third, and so on.

TABLE 6.6 – PAIRED COMPARISON OF PREMIUM SCHEDULE

Option	Premium	Deductible	Savings over previous option	Additional risk
	£	£	£	£
1	400.00	0	–	–
2	290.00	100	110.00	100
3	240.50	250	49.50	150
4	191.75	500	48.75	250
5	137.50	5000	54.25	4500
6	65.00	10000	72.50	5000

Table 6.6 displays the elements of the choices which the risk manager has to make. The choice between option 1 and 2 is a saving of £110 for additional risk of £100. In this case the additional risk would seem to be well worthwhile, in which case the choice between 2 and 3 is considered. If the risk manager believes the additional risk of £150 is worth £49.50 then he prefers the savings and will choose option 3. Comparing 3 with 4 reveals a smaller saving for a larger risk. If option 4 is acceptable then this is compared with 5 and in this case there is a small increase in savings but for a very much larger risk. If this is unacceptable then option 4 is the deductible level selected.

To illustrate the benefit of access to information regarding loss experience consider the premium schedule for property cover in Table 6.7.

Table 6.7 – PREMIUM SCHEDULE: PROPERTY EXPOSURE

Option	Premium	Deductible	Savings over previous option	Additional risk
	£	£	£	£
1	1135000	–	–	–
2	1000000	330000	135000	330000
3	470000	530000	530000	200000
4	–	4000000	470000	3470000

The comparisons have been outlined in Table 6.7. The additional information that is now to hand is the probabilities of occurrence of varying levels of loss which are drawn from the distribution of total losses. These probabilities are reproduced in Table 6.8.

Table 6.8 – EXPECTED LOSSES

Option	Risk	Additional risk	Probability of occurrence	Expected loss
	£	£	£	£
1	–	–	–	–
2	330000	330000	0.261	86130
3	530000	200000	0.50	100000
4	4000000	3470000	0.239	829330

The probability of occurrence column shows that there is a 26.1% chance of losses being less than £330,000; a 50% chance of losses falling between £330,000 and £530,000; and a 23.9% chance of losses exceeding £530,000.

In analysing the choice between options the manager can see that there is a premium saving of £135,000 from accepting a £330,000 deductible. This exposure has an expected value of £86,130. To accept the deductible is comparable to a decision to pay £135,000 for insurance on a £330,000 loss exposure with an expected value of £86,130. If this trade-off is acceptable, the manager can consider the next pairing of options in a similar manner. The choice between options 2 and 3 is an additional saving in premium of £530,000 for additional expected risk of £100,000 (£200,000 x 0.5) which may again prove attractive. The final choice yields an additional premium saving of £470,000 for an additional expected loss of £829,330. The risk here however may prove too great in which case the organisation would settle for the £530,000 deductible.

6.4.3 Statistical Analysis

Least cost and paired comparison are methods or tools to be applied in circumstances where reliable loss data does not exist or where the necessary expertise is not available. The least cost rule requires only the average incidence rate and as we have seen paired comparison can be utilised in the absence of loss data although if it is available it can assist the decision.

If however the data and the expertise are available it is possible to carry out a more thorough analysis to determine the appropriate deductible by means of the approach described by Professor G Dickinson in the *Handbook of Risk Management.*

The aim of this approach is to estimate the total financial cost of assuming a particular level of deductible for a forthcoming period of cover. This involves forecasting losses arising from the exposure concerned for the incoming year in layers or bands of losses. The starting point is the loss history of the organisation for the particular exposure which is reproduced in Table 6.9.

Table 6.9 – LOSSES FOR A 3-YEAR PERIOD
(adjusted for inflation)

Year	Losses £
1	182250
2	159250
3	296500

The next step is to break these costs down according to the size of loss ranging from zero to the maximum size of loss as shown in table 6.10. Note that the number of units of exposure which have not suffered loss are also included in the analysis.

Table 6.10

Size of loss £	Total	Annual[1] Average	Relative[1] Frequency
0	123	41.00	0.82
1 to 10000	16	5.33	0.107
10001 to 20000	4	1.33	0.027
20001 to 40000	3	1.00	0.02
40001 to 80000	1	0.33	0.007
80001 to 120000	2	0.67	0.013
120001 and greater	1	0.33	0.007
	150	50.00	1.000

[1] Does not add due to rounding

Distribution of Losses Over a Three Year Period

Table 6.10 shows the distribution of losses over the three-year period. The average number of units subject to the exposure each year has also been calculated. The relative frequency is determined by dividing the frequency of occurrence within each of the layers of loss by the total number of exposures. Thus the relative frequency for units involving no loss is 123/150 = 0.82. If the annual average figures were used the result would be the same: 41/50 = 0.82.

Relative frequency relates to past losses but under certain circumstances can be used as a measure of probability. Used in this way the relative frequencies that have been calculated enable the number of occurrences within each layer of loss for the forthcoming period to be determined. Note that changes in the legislative and technological environments and other changes which alter the conditions under which the organisation will be operating over the incoming period cannot be reflected in these figures. It would be necessary in these circumstances to note a qualification on results derived from probabilities to this effect.

For the purposes of the example however we shall assume that any changes can be incorporated in the figures. Specifically, the number of units is increased to 60 and inflation over the period is expected to be 5% p.a. As there is a larger number of exposures it is reasonable to expect there will be a larger number of occurrences. This is found by multiplying the increased number of units by the probabilities that have been derived from the relative frequencies.

The losses also have to be adjusted to allow for the inflationary factor over the incoming period. Before undertaking this it is important to ensure that the historical loss data has been adjusted to current prices and that the losses are expressed in latest year prices; thereafter the inflation factor can be applied. For the purposes of this analysis it is necessary to calculate the average loss for each loss layer. This and not the mid-point of the loss layer is the figure used to determine the total loss arising in each layer. The results of these calculations are presented in Table 6.11.

Table 6.11

Size of loss	Probability[1]	Expected[1] occurrences	Average loss	Total loss per layer
£			£	£
0	0.82	49.20	–	–
1 to 10000	0.107	6.42	3940	25295
10001 to 20000	0.027	1.62	13650	22113
20001 to 40000	0.02	1.20	30450	36540
40001 to 80000	0.007	0.42	42260	17749
80001 to 120000	0.013	0.78	104340	81385
more than 120001	0.007	0.42	210000	88200
	1.000	60.00		

[1] Does not add due to rounding

Determining the Total Loss Arising in Each Layer

The total loss per layer is found by multiplying the adjusted frequency by the average loss for each layer. This information can then be used to calculate the cost of losses falling under each deductible.

The cost of retained losses under each deductible is equal to the sum of each of the losses which are less than the deductible plus the deductible assumed for each of those losses which are greater than the deductible. To illustrate: if a £20,000 deductible is assumed, the cost of the retained losses is:

losses from £1 to £10,000	£25,295	
losses from £10,001 to £20,000	22,113	£47,408
losses greater than £20,000		56,400
(2.82 x £20,000)		103,808

This calculation is carried out for each deductible level. Given the premium and deductible schedule from the insurer we are now in a position to identify the level of deductible which maximises the difference between the savings in premium and the costs of retention. The results are presented in Table 6.12. Administration costs have been included to reflect the increased administrative burden of assuming additional levels of deductible.

Table 6.12 – SUMMARY OF TOTAL COSTS AND NET SAVINGS

Premium	Deductible	Retained losses	Admin. costs	Total costs	Net savings
£	£	£	£	£	£
200000	–	–	–	200000	–
100000	10000	69695	2500	172195	27805
60000	20000	103808	3500	167308	32692
35000	40000	148748	5000	188748	11252
29000	80000	197697	7500	234197	(34197)
24000	120000	233481	11000	268481	(68481)
15000	160000	271282	15000	301282	(101282)

The Difference Between the Savings in Promotion and the Costs of Retention

The total costs are made up of retained losses plus administration costs. Net savings is the difference between the total costs of full cover (£200,000) and the total costs of the various levels of deductible.

6.4.4 The Modified Houston Model

Professor D B Houston, writing in 1964, proposed a model to compare the effect of two methods of financing pure risk costs upon the value of an organisation. The methods examined were full insurance cover of the exposure and full retention losses arising out of the exposure. The model was subsequently modified by Professor M Greene and Professor O Serbein to incorporate a deductible decision model. The analysis by Professors Greene and Serbein is based on an aggregate or stop loss deductible.

The value of the organisation is defined in terms of net worth, the effect of various levels of deductible being judged on the basis of the effect which they have upon the organisation's ability to safeguard and increase this figure. The net worth of an organisation is the difference between its assets and its liabilities. As such it is a measure of the value of the owners' or shareholders' stake in the organisation. The insurance or retention decision has implications for the net worth of the enterprise as expenditure on insurance or retention reduces the funds or assets available to the organisation to engage in its profit-making activities. For example if the net worth of an enterprise was £120 million and it expects to earn a rate of return on its assets during the year of 16% its value at the end of the trading period will be £139.2 million.

However as the organisation has property exposure it has to make provisions to finance the losses when they occur. If it purchases insurance at say £600,000 in respect of property value at £30 million this reduces the assets on which the return can be earned, with the result that its net worth is reduced to £138.504 million, a reduction of £0.696 million. This can be summarised in the following formula:

$$FP_1 = NW - P + r\,(NW - P)$$

where FP_1 is the financial position of an organisation at the end of its financial period insuring its exposures

      NW   is the net worth of the organisation at the beginning of the financial period

      P   is the insurance premium

      r   is the average rate of return on assets employed

The effect upon net worth of wholly retaining the risk can be determined in a similar fashion. Thus:

$$FP_R = NW - L + r\,(NW - L - F) + iF$$

where FP_R is the financial position of an organisation at the end of its financial period wholly retaining losses arising from its exposure

      L   is the expected losses

      F   is the reserve fund

      i   is the rate of interest on financial assets held in reserve fund

In addition to the expected losses which the organisation will have to finance, funds have also been set aside in a reserve fund to provide sufficient liquidity in order to guard against fluctuations in actual from expected losses. It is assumed that the assets held in the fund are more liquid in nature and therefore earn a lower rate of return.

If we assume that expected losses are £500,000 for the year, that the rate of return on financial assets is 10% p.a. and that from previous experience the reserve fund requires to be 15% of the sums insured, the financial position of the organisation, if it fully retains its property exposure, is:

$$
\begin{aligned}
FP_R = \ & 120,000,000 - 500,000 + \\
& 0.16(120,000,000 - 500,000 - 4,500,000) + \\
& 0.1(4,500,000)
\end{aligned}
$$

$$= \ 119,500,000 + 18,400,000 + 450,000$$

$$= \ 138,350,000$$

Recalling the financial position of the organisation with insurance was £138,504,000 we can see that on this occasion at least it is better off through purchasing insurance to finance its property losses.

Before proceeding to consider how the model can be modified to incorporate a deductible it is worthwhile to note that this formulation does not consider:

- the effect of the timing and settlement of losses;

- the effect of the time value of money. This latter point could be incorporated in a revised version of the formula but this is beyond our purposes for the moment.

The formula to determine the financial position of the organisation with an aggregate deductible is:

$$FP_D = NW - Pd - kD + r(NW - Pd - kD - F) + iF$$

where FP_D is the financial position of an organisation at the end of its financial period partially self-financing exposures by means of aggregate deductible

      Pd is the deductible premium

      kD is the expected losses under the deductible

To illustrate, we assume that the aggregate deductible is £1,000,000, the corresponding premium is £350,000 and that the reserve fund has been set at £1,000,000. The only unknown is the size of expected losses beneath the deductible. This in turn depends on the value of k which is based on the discount offered by the insurer. The value of k is derived in the following way:

1. Calculate the pure risk premium, thus:

$$\text{premium} \times (1 - \text{expense ratio})$$

From the example £600,000 (0.75) = £450,000

2. Calculate insurer's discount, thus:

$$\frac{\text{full premium} - \text{deductible premium}}{\text{full premium}} \times \frac{100}{1}$$

$$\frac{£600,000 - £350,000}{£600,000} \times 100 = 42\%$$

3. Calculate the pure risk transferred under the deductible, thus:

    pure risk premium x premium discount
    0.42 (£450,000) = £189,000

4. Express k as a fraction of the deductible:

$$\frac{£189,000 \times 100}{£1,000,000} = 0.189$$

The rationale of this approach is that the insurer is prepared to offer a discount to the insured in return for the insured accepting some of the losses that the insurer would otherwise have had to meet. It is assumed that the discount the insurer offers will reflect the amount of risk that is being transferred (or returned) to the insured. In the above case the discount amounted to 42% of the full premium which implied that 42% of all losses fell within the £1,000,000 deductible. The full premium however included expenses and other loadings which were assumed to account for 25% of the premium. Thus the pure risk premium was £450,000. Since the pure risk premium is set in order to recover claims costs this represents the expected cost of losses for the year. According to our calculations 42% of these costs or £189,000 has to be borne by the insured under the aggregate deductible.

We now have all the information necessary to apply the formula in respect of the deductible. Thus:

$$
\begin{aligned}
\text{FP}_\text{D} &= £120,000,000 - 350,000 - 189,000 + \\
&\quad 0.16(120,000,000 - 350,000 - 189,000 - \\
&\quad 1,000,000) + 0.1(1,000,000) \\
&= £119,461,000 + 18,954,000 + 100,000 \\
&= £138,515,000
\end{aligned}
$$

The assumption of the £1,000,000 deductible is preferred in this case to either of the options of full insurance or full retention considered earlier because it yields a higher net worth position.

In theory it would be possible to determine the maximum premium for any level of deductible or alternatively establish the appropriate level of deductible for any level of premium. In practice since the market usually offers only a limited number of deductible levels it may not be possible to purchase the package which gives the most preferred distribution of risk as indicated by the model. However it is possible to derive the maximum acceptable premium given a particular deductible.

This would be found by setting FP_1 equal to FP_D and solving for Pd. Drawing from our example:

$$£138,504,000 = £120,000,000 - 189,000 - Pd +$$
$$0.16(119,811,000 - 1,000,000 - Pd) +$$
$$0.1(1,000,000)$$

$$= £138,920,000 - Pd\ (1 + 0.16)$$

$$Pd\ (1.16) = £138,920,000 - 138,504,000 = £416,000$$

$$Pd = £416,000/1.16$$

$$= £358,620.69$$

6.5 CONCLUSION

The deductible involves the financing of risk by the organisation that would previously have been assumed by the insurer but within the overall context of insurance cover. They are suited to dealing with loss layers which are predictable and relatively stable and which insurers have been glad to transfer because of the disproportionate amount of administration required, relative to the size of the claims.

Strategically, deductibles can be used by a parent company in conjunction with a funded reserve or a captive to provide the financing of a group deductible on a scale that would not be appropriate to individual subsidiary companies. However the combined size and spread of the exposures could well provide conditions suitable to the retention of significant portions of some of their exposures. The deductible can be operated at group level sharing the risk with the insurer and at local level through local deductibles financed through a funded reserve or a captive insurer appropriate to the resources of the subsidiaries. Deductibles therefore can be used by an organisation to participate in the financing of its own exposures without exposing its own financial resources to catastrophic loss.

7

CAPTIVES (1)
NATURE, FORMATION AND
FEASIBILITY

7.1 INTRODUCTION

The establishment of a captive insurance company is in effect the formalisation of an organisation's self-funding provisions. Full consideration of the risk management and financial implications is therefore required prior to its formation. Once operational a wide range of additional formal requirements and responsibilities are assumed. Nevertheless the number of organisations which have taken this route has been increasing especially over the past twenty to thirty years.

A captive insurance company is:

> "a limited purpose, wholly owned insurance subsidiary of an organisation not in the insurance business, which has as its primary function the insuring of some of the exposures and risks of its parent or parent's affiliates."

More succinctly it has been defined as the insurance subsidiary of a non-insurance parent writing all or part of the risks of the parent.

Some authors have traced the captive principle to mutual schemes for financial protection organised by the trade guilds of the Middle Ages and mutual groups in the nineteenth century. The first captives of the modern era which emerged during the 1920s and 1930s in Europe and the UK were founded by companies such as ICI, Unilever and BP. Today there are well over 3,000 captives worldwide.

The majority of the growth has been in captives of US parentage, starting in the 1950s but gathering pace from the late 1960s to the 1980s. The rate of growth in captive formation has been related to the underwriting cycle in the insurance market. In recent times captives have become more feasible for smaller entities.

US captives have generally been formed to provide cover in the area of casualty insurance, specifically product liability and professional negligence. In Europe, UK companies have been the most active in captive company formation although Dutch, Belgian and German companies – where captives have been part of the insurance market for a number of years – have also been active. Originally UK and European captives were usually formed to provide cover for property and material damage, however, today all types of conventional risks are insured by UK and European owned captives.

The growth in captives in both the US and Europe has been marked by the establishment of many of these companies in domiciles other than that of the parent – the 'offshore' location. Bermuda was and still remains the most popular with US companies but other centres such as Cayman Islands, Barbados, Channel Islands, Isle of Man, Gibraltar, Luxembourg, Hong Kong, Vanuatu and Nauru and Singapore are among those which have developed. Table 7.1 provides a fuller list of these centres.

Onshore locations have developed where existing legislation has made it difficult to form offshore captives such as in Germany or where legislation has been enacted as in Vermont and other states in the US to facilitate the establishment of such companies.

Table 7.1 – CAPTIVE LOCATIONS

Bahamas	Gibraltar	Nauru
Netherlands	Guernsey	US Virgin Islands
Antilles	Hong Kong	Singapore
Barbados	Isle of Man	Turks and Caicos
Bermuda	Jersey	Tennessee
Cayman Islands	Luxembourg	Vanuatu
Colorado	Malta	Vermont
Cyprus		

7.2 REASONS FOR FORMATION

A substantial number of reasons are cited by a range of authors. These usually fall into two main areas:

(i) dissatisfaction with conventional insurance markets; and

(ii) the 'advantages' of a captive.

The captive must be seen as part of the overall risk management process. A company which loses sight of this and the necessity for sound risk analysis, reduction and control measures will find the captive a short-lived and expensive venture.

7.2.1 Dissatisfaction with the Conventional Markets

The main points which emerge are:

- volatility of insurance prices and capacity;
- inequitable rating structures;
- unavailability of cover;
- inflexibility of conventional wordings in the conventional insurance market;
- concerns about insurer security;
- inadequate service.

7.2.1.1 Market Volatility

The swings in the insurance underwriting cycle that have been experienced in recent years have increased rather than reduced uncertainty. Substantial movements in premium rates or unexpected withdrawal of capacity from the market have made it more difficult to provide continuity in risk financing arrangements.

Establishing an insurance subsidiary enables the organisation to price insurance based on its own loss experience. This permits the organisation to develop a long term rating structure, partly in isolation from the vagaries of the insurance markets, and provide continuity in risk financing costs that, by comparison with the conventional markets, can prove attractive.

7.2.1.2 The Rating Structure

Whilst the principle of insurance is the sharing of the losses of the few among the many, insurance buyers are reluctant to continue to subsidise the poor loss experience of others on a long term basis. Premium rating is based on average loss, but if an organisation has a loss experience consistently below the average whilst others are consistently in excess of it, it is effectively subsidising poor loss control practices. It is understandable that a buyer should wish to opt out of such an arrangement, especially if the insurer fails to recognise and reward good loss experience.

7.2.1.3 Availability of Cover

The market has in the past been unwilling to continue to provide cover at sufficiently high levels of exposure following the occurrence of claims, particularly in the product and environmental liability areas. Where it has been made available its value and effectiveness has been restricted by policy wordings.

Captives such as ACE (American Casualty Excess) offering cover for liabilities in excess of $100m; Excel offering cover for the layer for $50m to $100m; and COIL Ltd providing excess facilities for oil pollution liability cover have been formed as a direct response to the inadequacy of conventional market capacity.

In addition, there are some areas of exposure, such as industrial action, where insurers are unable to offer cover due to regulatory restraints on policy wordings.

Inflexibility of conventional wordings in the conventional insurance market

The existence and development of claims made wordings and current lack of ability to secure long term insurance arrangements has resulted in some insureds questioning the long term value of entering into an annual relationship with an insurer.

7.2.1.4 Underwriting Rates

Certain areas of exposure such as product liability have been subject to sharp and ultimately unjustifiable increases in rate, if in fact the cover has been available at all.

Underwriters have been nervous about writing business where there is an insufficient spread of risk or where there is a lack of technical information relating to the exposure. Necessity has forced organisations to deal with these kinds of risk outwith the insurance markets.

7.2.1.5 Quality of Ancillary Services

Organisations have moved to the use of the captive in a bid to improve or at least have more control over the quality and delivery of the ancillary services such as claims management and control, loss reduction and control, and technical support.

This step has freed the organisation from the insurer as the sole provider of these services and allows it to buy them independently of insurance cover, either from independent specialist providers of such services or insurers on a fee-related basis.

7.2.2 Benefits from Captive Formation

These are generally accepted to be:

- savings in insurance costs;
- selection of risks;
- risk control;
- supplement to conventional market cover;
- access to reinsurance markets;
- limited taxation benefits;
- benefits of offshore insurance locations;
- implementation of global risk financing strategy;
- development as a profit centre.

These points are not presented in any order of merit, although the facility to control losses and risk financing strategy are frequently mentioned. It has to be noted that many of the operational advantages listed would also be available from an internal fund.

7.2.2.1 Insurance Savings

Use of the captive means that the organisation is able to avoid contributing to the costs of the insurer such as its clerical, accounting and other expenses which are normally a fixed charge and do not usually reflect the usage of the insurer's services by the buyer. In addition the captive does not require to incur the marketing costs of acquiring new business or contribute towards insurers' profits.

If the loss experience of the parent is better than the average in the market then further savings arise in this area. Furthermore, placing the risk with the captive means that since premium is retained, the captive is able to enjoy the cash flow benefits arising from control of the funds until settlement of losses is required.

The cost of insurance is also reduced as cover can be purchased in the reinsurance market at lower cost.

7.2.2.2 Selection of Risks

Risks can be retained by the captive or transferred to direct insurers. This can be applied in the first instance to various classes of exposures. Those with relatively predictable experience would be obvious candidates for retention. After having decided how much of the lower level claims to retain, the captive manager will buy reinsurance cover above this level.

Selection can also be made within an individual class of risk according to experience or financial capacity of the captive. For example a petrochemical company may be content to retain the property risk on its retail outlets because of the spread of risk and relatively low severity of loss, but wish to maintain insurance cover for the small number of high-value refineries it operates and optimise the risk financing strategy by benefiting from both its superior loss experience over the retail outlets and the market system of common rating for the refinery exposure.

7.2.2.3 Risk Control

Retaining risk means that the impact of loss experience is felt immediately. Improvement or deterioration in the parent's loss experience will be reflected in the underwriting results of the captive.

By externalising and isolating the cost of the organisation's pure risk in this manner, the risk manager may also be able to use the captive to enforce and demonstrate the benefits of loss control. This can also provide motivation for the pursuit of the benefits to be derived from a full risk management policy.

7.2.2.4 Supplement to Conventional Markets

You will recall from Section 7.2.1.3 that part of the impetus for the development of captives was lack of cover in the conventional market.

In principle the captive is able to create funds which can be used to fund losses arising from a contingent event and thereby insure risks for which the conventional market is unable to offer full coverage.

7.2.2.5 Access to Reinsurance

The reinsurance markets are wholesale insurance markets with the reinsurers operating as wholesalers. As such they do not have to maintain the same branch network as retailers nor do they have the same scale of head office operations. Consequently their cost structure is lower. The average sum insured or liability covered is also significantly larger. The benefit to the buyer is lower costs per unit of cover.

Moreover, in contrast to the direct market, the reinsurance market has been ready to give more control to the buyer over the amount of risk retained or reinsured by being prepared to relate premiums more directly to loss experience, to be more flexible in their attitude towards underwriting unusual risks, or to offer cover with a substantial deductible on an excess of loss basis.

7.2.2.6 Taxation

In many cases the tax benefits from a captive are in the first instance the tax deductibility of premiums paid to it. Historically a lower rate of corporate or profits tax (which in some 'offshore' locations is zero) than that ruling in the domicile of the parent was possible. The lower rates levied against underwriting profits and investment income enabled the captive's reserves and therefore its risk bearing capacity to be built up more quickly. Today, however, the situation globally is quite different with international tax laws tightening and an increasing trend moving towards taxation of global profits.

Payment of contributions to the captive can, provided certain conditions are satisfied, be set against tax thus reducing the cost to the parent and placing them on the same footing as insurance premiums. In the US tax deductions can be secured if the captive transaction is at arms length and the captive is a brother/sister company to the premium paying entity, i.e. risk is shifted from one balance sheet to another albeit within the same economic family.

The UK position is that tax deductibility of premiums paid to a captive will be allowed provided the captive can demonstrate to the satisfaction of the Inland Revenue that it is a genuine insurance subsidiary operating at 'arms length' and not a mechanism for the diversion of profits from the UK and thus the reduction or avoidance of tax. The tax position of the captive of a UK parent is discussed at greater length in the next chapter.

7.2.2.7 Offshore Locations

In addition to the lower local rates of corporate tax, the regulatory environment in the offshore locations is also less stringent than those ruling in the domicile of the parent. This means that the captive can be set up more speedily and with less cost than in the more heavily regulated environment. A number of States in the US notably Vermont, Colorado and Hawaii have also enacted legislation to encourage the establishment of such insurance subsidiaries.

7.2.2.8 Global Risk Financing Strategy

Within major multinationals there is often a desire to retain as much risk as possible in relation to its overall financial position. Where there is a decentralised structure conflicts of view can arise between group and local management upon the amount of risk that should be retained. The result could be that the worldwide insurance costs are greater than they should be and that the level of risk retained is not related to the financial strength of the organisation.

The captive can play a part in centralising a worldwide risk financing policy by obtaining business from the insurers handling the country's subsidiary insurance programmes, so that the profits previously accruing to the insurers now accrue to the captive. In addition global insurance programmes can be developed using one insurer or a consortium of insurers. Local coverage can then be supplemented through global policies retaining higher deductibles than those applying locally, and which can provide higher limits and wide ranges of cover than may be available in some countries where multinationals operate. The captive can provide additional flexibility when dealing with local technical difficulties such as regulation of policy wordings, local capacity and premium control. For example, if local insurance regulations prohibit the placing of business with a non-admitted or unauthorised insurer, the risks can be placed initially with a local insurer and reinsured through the captive.

The captive therefore can provide the means of achieving greater control over an organisation's overall risk financing strategy through the integration of local and group deductibles, the provision of wider coverage and the reduction of insurance expenditure.

7.2.2.9 Development as a Profit Centre

The successful operation of the captive adds value to the parent organisation as its pure risk costs are reduced through improved loss control and reduced risk financing costs. The profitable operation of the captive will enable it to continue and develop a fuller range of loss experience and growth in its reserves. The increase in financial resources and experience can allow it to enlarge the amount of risk it can afford to retain in several ways.

It can extend the cover that it offers to the parent by for example increasing the level of group deductible or expanding the number of exposures covered. It could also reduce the level of reinsurance protection that it purchases and retain more funds under its control. Continued profitability and maturity has also led a number of captives into providing cover for exposures outwith the ownership of the parent or its affiliates.

Some organisations have successfully used the captive structure to manage very specific third party customer risks such as warranty risk exposures. Recent changes to UK tax rules are likely to make this type of operation less attractive.

7.2.3 Problems Associated with Captive Formation

The main problems are:

- narrowness of the portfolio of exposures;
- costs of establishment and operation;
- co-operation with the direct insurance market;
- local insurance regulations;
- government controls over insurance companies;
- internal management pressures;
- sensitivity to poor loss experience;
- management time.

7.2.3.1 Narrowness of the Portfolio

The captive's limited and narrow range of loss experience particularly in the early stages of its development will reduce its ability to retain higher levels of risk and increase its need for insurance protection. If the spread of risk is low but the values are high the reinsurance costs may be so high that the amount left to fund the retention may be insufficient.

Moreover if the captive is considering insuring risks for which cover is not available in the market, there may be insufficient data to justify the level of premium set. This becomes especially problematic in the case of contingent liabilities such as strikes and product recall for which the organisation has little or no loss experience.

7.2.3.2 Establishment and Operating Costs

There is a wide range of costs additional to claims and reinsurance costs which have to be met by a captive. The initial or establishment costs are:

- minimum capitalisation requirements;
- stamp duty on capitalisation although this is often limited with a financial cap;
- registration fee;
- application fee;
- legal fees;
- advertising of the captive in compliance with legislative requirements;
- cost of feasibility study to support business plan.

Compliance with the regulatory requirements for the establishment of an insurance company imposes costs in terms of the minimum capitalisation required and the assets that must be held in order to meet solvency requirements. The reserving required for high value exposures will operate to the disadvantage of the establishment of the captive. Apart from the statutory requirements practitioners recommend that in the early years of its life, capitalisation should be at least 50% of premium income.

During the course of its life the captive has also to meet a number of recurring costs such as legal, directors, management (including fund management), audit and registration fees.

The reinsurance market tends to be experience-rated so that the loss history of the captive will be directly related to the reinsurance cost. The organisation's loss control capability will therefore be a crucial factor in this area. For example, where there is an insufficient margin between the risks retained by the captive and the funds withheld to finance them, any significant loss in a year could alter the position dramatically. Where funds were insufficient to meet the loss or had been eroded by poor loss experience the captive would fail.

7.2.3.3 Co-operation from the Direct Market

Co-operation from the direct market in the form of fronting facilities, engineering and claims facilities may not be available in difficult market conditions or may be costly. Moreover reinsurance facilities for normally uninsurable risks may not be available.

7.2.3.4 Local Insurance Regulations

These may impose restriction on:

- the availability of fronting facilities by restricting the amounts of premium that can be remitted to a captive;
- controls on reserve requirements;
- controls on placing of reinsurance business, for example with the state-owned reinsurer;
- controls on the types of investment that the captive can hold.

7.2.3.5 Government Controls

Government controls in the parent's domicile over insurers with respect to their solvency, capitalisation, exchange control, reserve assets, and authorisation requirements such as performance, statutory returns and the like will inhibit the establishment of the subsidiary. Furthermore, legislation may prohibit or severely restrict formation of the captive in an alternative location.

7.2.3.6 Internal Management Pressure

As the captive is a subsidiary of the parent, management within the company may see the opportunity to place pressure on captive management in a way that would not have been possible if dealing with an ordinary insurer – for example to adopt a more favourable attitude in the settlement, particularly of liability claims, or alter the premium rating structure to reduce risk financing costs in particular areas.

7.2.3.7 Loss Experience

The financial viability of the captive rests ultimately on the loss experience and therefore the risk management and loss control capability of the parent. The parent is not insulated from poor loss experience in the same way as it is when insured in the direct market as this is reflected in the results of the captive.

7.2.3.8 Management Costs

Finally, a factor that may be overlooked is the substantial amount of management time that is required to be devoted at the outset to the issues surrounding the establishment and operation of the captive. Even if the actual study of the feasibility of the proposal can be performed by external consultants and the management of the captive contracted out to a management company, the considerable amount of time that still has to be expended by senior management may not be justified in relation to the return that the parent can expect from the captive.

7.3 TYPES OF CAPTIVE

The definition of a captive that we gave at the beginning of the chapter does not indicate the different forms in which captives can take. They differ according to size, parentage, scope of operation, function and location.

7.3.1 Ownership

The captive can be owned exclusively by a single company or jointly by a group of companies or other organisations. They are referred to as single-parent and multi-parent captives respectively.

7.3.1.1 Single-parent Captives

Most UK owned captives fall into this category. The main benefits are that the parent is free to decide on the objectives of the captive, loss experience is confidential to the parent, and the captive is able to control its own affairs.

7.3.1.2 Multi-parent Captives

A multi-parent captive enables the pooling of risks on a mutual basis. It is an arrangement which is more popular in the US. The advantage is that both the risk-bearing capacity of the captive and the spread of risk is increased.

The results are that it provides a facility to handle risks that would be beyond the capacity of an individual member, increases the buying power and negotiating position with the market place, spreads the management costs among the members, and makes it less likely that funds paid to the captive in respect of contributions to the fund will be challenged by the tax authorities as there is an element of risk transfer taking place. The mutual basis of the multi-parent arrangement opens the captive route to organisations which by virtue of insufficient premium or spread of risk would not be able to justify the formation of a captive on their own account.

The multi-parent arrangement is not without its problems. It requires the co-operation between organisations whose management standards are known to each other and which share similar concerns and areas of exposure. Inevitably there is a loss of confidentiality in respect to loss experience and also a loss of freedom in the objectives set for the captive. It is likely that more management time will be taken up in discussion with the partners than would be the case in the single-parent company, and there is also the possibility of conflict of interests through disagreements over policy or poor loss experience of one of the partners.

Association captives are similar in organisation and purpose to multi-parent captives. They are distinguished from multi-parent captives in that they are established by professional bodies, trade associations and other similar bodies.

Protected Cell Captives (PCCs)

Protected cell captives are a relatively new development. Basically a PCC is a single legal entity with segregated cells which provide users with a ringfenced participation. One cell is not exposed to the risks of the other cell. A core cell provides support to the cells and is owned by a separate party. Hence PCCs are not to mutualise risk, rather they provide a low cost ready made captive facility for new captive entrants. PCC legislation has been introduced in many domiciles. In some domiciles the reference is to a segregated portfolio or segregated account company rather than a PCC.

A PCC has a single set of accounts and has cellular and no-cellular assets. The cells themselves are not legal entities, can survive the insolvency of the PCC and can be migrated to another host PCC.

The legal, tax and accounting position for PCCs is complex and subject to continued speculation/development.

PCCs are an ideal vehicle for a smaller captive programme.

7.3.2 Scope of Operation

A captive can operate on either a pure or open-market footing.

A pure captive is one which underwrites only its parent's business. Most captives are established on this basis.

7.3.2.1 Open-market Captive

An open-market captive will, in addition to its parent's business, write cover for exposures that are not owned by the parent – unrelated business. The principal means by which the open-market captive can write unrelated business is by participation in a reinsurance pool or through a reciprocal insurance exchange.

The reinsurance pool permits the captive to participate in the risks of other captives and reinsurers. The pool is usually managed by an underwriting agency or an insurance company and carries the attraction that participation is relatively straightforward and no underwriting experience is required on the part of the captive. This however can also be a disadvantage in that the captive has no control over or awareness of or ability to assess the underwriting standards of the pool. Participation in a pool with poor underwriting standards can be an expensive business.

The objective of a reciprocal insurance exchange is to expand the base and spread of risk of the captive without reducing its profitability and to give it access to business that would otherwise be unobtainable due to its limited risk bearing capacity. The captive exchanges a portion of its exposures with another captive or insurer on the basis that the business subject to the arrangement is equally profitable on either side.

It is important that the necessary underwriting expertise is available within the captive as the obvious need here is to ensure that both companies' performances are similar.

7.3.3 Function

A captive can function on either a direct or reinsurance basis. A captive operating on a direct basis issues policies direct to its clients, whereas a reinsurance captive will operate through a fronting insurer which will deal with policy issues.

A direct captive is limited in the business it can write as many countries restrict the writing of some or all classes of business to authorised or admitted insurers which conform to the statutory requirements of the territory concerned. A captive operating on a direct basis would be largely excluded from such markets. Short of establishing a captive in each of these countries which will be impractical in the majority of cases, the parent will require to purchase cover in the local market which calls into question the original role of the captive.

The majority of captives therefore participate in the parent's risks through reinsuring the risks from an admitted insurer operating in the local market on its behalf, providing there are no restrictions upon the placing of reinsurance outside the local market. This is referred to as fronting and to a multi-national it may prove to be the only practicable means for the captive to share in the risks of the parent.

7.3.4 Location

We have already indicated that many captives are located offshore for reasons such as low local tax rates and a less onerous legislative environment. Nevertheless some captives are situated in a domestic location. The element of the organisational convenience is one factor quoted by organisations that have taken this step. The legislative framework may make it more difficult to establish an offshore captive there may be political reasons for retaining the captive or domestically, for example the organisation could be partially or wholly owned by the government.

7.4 FEASIBILITY STUDY

The formation of a captive represents a major commitment of time and resources and should not be entered into lightly. Its use has to be justified in relation to alternative risk financing techniques – some of which are examined in other chapters – and should only be adopted if the study demonstrates that it provides a net advantage to the management of the pure risks of the parent. To this end the establishment of the insurance subsidiary should be the subject of a feasibility study. This can be carried out either by internal staff or externally by brokers or consultants.

If the study is to be performed in-house, it will require a team comprising expertise drawn from a number of areas. The team should include legal, financial, taxation and risk management staff and be led by the risk manager. Although this has the benefit of using staff who are well versed in the activities of the organisation as well as their own area of expertise, it is also particularly demanding on staff time. For this reason the task is often delegated to brokers or consultants, who although not having the in-depth knowledge of the organisation possessed by internal staff, are able to draw upon the expertise and knowledge of staff experienced in these areas. To ensure objectivity of analysis, remuneration should be fee-based and not linked to the recommendations of the study.

The discipline of undertaking the study is also useful in that it provides a framework for the operation of the company in the event that it is established.

Practitioners vary in their approach to such an exercise but of necessity there are a number of areas which have to be examined:

- the objectives of the parent for the captive;
- the loss and insurance history of the parent;
- the current spread of exposure;
- the operational requirements and implications of the captive.

7.4.1 Pre-conditions of Captive Formation

These areas are examined to determine whether in the first instance the necessary pre-conditions for the establishment of the captive are satisfied. This will include projected performance of the captive under a number of scenarios, including a worst case position.

Bawcutt in *Captive Insurance Companies* (Witherby & Co Ltd) details the pre-conditions as:

- that the parent has a satisfactory loss control capability;

- that senior management is aware of and understands the implications of such a step and is fully committed to it;

- that the level of risk to be retained on each exposure and for the captive as a whole has been determined. As the level of risk retention is often related to corporate attitude to risk in general it is necessary that the captive should also reflect this attitude;

- that there is sufficient premium volume. The minimum level is normally set between £250,000 and £500,000 depending on the nature of the exposure. For example low severity high frequency exposures may be set at the lower end of this range. This volume of premium is required because of the management costs that have to be paid in addition to claims. Below this level it will probably be more economic to use alternative risk financing techniques;

- that the co-operation of the direct and reinsurance markets is available;

- that the captive's management understand its needs with respect to establishment and operation and recognise when external advice and assistance should be sought.

This study is often made in two stages: the first being an overview of the current insurance arrangements and loss experience of previous years, the range of exposures and comments about unsatisfactory features of the current arrangements. The second will contain an in-depth study of the loss history, methods and effectiveness of loss control, projections of captive performance under various conditions and comparisons with alternative risk financing arrangements.

7.4.2 Objectives

Prior to embarking upon the study it is essential to ascertain why the parent is considering this step. A study of the motivation for the formation of US captives in 1981 revealed the results shown in Table 7.2.

Table 7.2 – MAJOR OBJECTIVES CITED FOR ESTABLISHING CAPTIVES

	Percentage of Respondents Indicating Objective Was Very Important (Per cent)
Four Main Objectives:	
1. To reduce insurance costs	73
2. To facilitate obtaining insurance coverage	55
3. To obtain more favourable insurance terms and conditions	55
4. To increase profits on funds held for payment of losses	48
Seven Less Important Objectives:	
1. To enable corporate cash flow	29
2. To obtain appropriate credits for assuming deductibles	29
3. To encourage more and better corporate loss control	27
4. To obtain income tax advantages	10
5. To facilitate handling insurance on foreign operations	10
6. To enter insurance business – serve third parties	10
7. To increase importance of risk manager's job	5

Reproduced with permission from M R Greene, O N Serbein
Risk Management: Text and Cases p 139
Reston Publishing, Reston, Virginia USA 1983

Bawcutt in *Captive Insurance Companies* lists the following objectives:

    (i)   to reduce insurance costs;

(ii) to improve existing coverage or to provide cover for risks which are currently uninsurable;

(iii) to satisfy risk financing needs;

(iv) to obtain adequate credit for more self-insurance;

(v) to integrate multi-national insurance programmes;

(vi) to improve cash flow;

(vii) to help implement group risk management or risk financing strategy;

(viii) to diversify from core business or create an insurance profit centre.

The function of the objectives is to set the standard by which the feasibility of the captive is to be judged and determine the level of detail required by the study. Thus if the objective is to reduce insurance costs, this sets less onerous requirements than those implied by an objective to establish the captive as a separate profit centre that will eventually expand into unrelated business.

7.4.3 Loss History

A detailed investigation of claims paid by the insurer and loss retained by the parent, whether under a loss sharing arrangement with the insurer such as a deductible or a wholly retained risk, will have to be carried out. If possible data for the previous five years in the case of liability losses and for the previous ten years in the case of property losses should be obtained for analysis. Historical data has to be adjusted for inflation and other quantifiable changes such as workforce, sales turnover, vehicles, area, etc, to ensure that as far as possible it is directly comparable to current figures.

Whilst it is not possible to incorporate qualitative changes such as changes in markets, technology, standards of loss prevention, and management attitudes to the management of risk amongst others in the analysis, they should be noted and their effect, if any, recognised.

Information from retained losses can be used to analyse the loss experience under certain levels of deductible in order to assess the impact of various levels of retention upon the captive.

Investigation of claims should include whether any loss prevention measures such as sprinklers, machine guards, alarms, etc were in use and whether there have been any changes in management attitude to and the practice of loss control over the period under review.

7.4.4 Existing Insurance Programme

Details of premiums, premium discounts and cover for all classes of business for the previous five to ten years have to be gathered. Premium data has to be adjusted for inflation in order that it is expressed in current values. Where a change in premium is due to changes in the terms of the cover this should be noted. The extent of discounts which have been offered by the market in respect of various levels of deductible and other risk sharing arrangements should also be noted.

The location of the parent's operations will have to be considered, in particular the number and identity of countries in which it operates, as this will influence the choice of insurer to provide fronting and reinsurance facilities. Local insurance regulations should be examined to establish the locations in which the captive can operate on a non-admitted basis, the level of self-insurance that could be operated at local level and the practicability of incorporating all countries within the captive programme. The details relating to the operation of non-admitted insurers such as premium levels, tariff rating restraints, the extent of policy cover available and whether premium taxes are levied should be obtained. These factors are of importance as they can affect the financial viability of the captive.

In many countries the captive will not be able to operate directly and will therefore require the services of a fronting insurer. The study should ascertain whether there are constraints upon the amount of business that must be retained by the insurer and also the restrictions on the amount that can be reinsured to the captive. Attention should also be given to the remittance arrangements for the reinsurance premiums, specifically the timing of these and any delays that may be anticipated.

The analysis of the programme also has to take account of current market conditions, that is the phase the market has reached in the underwriting cycle, to ascertain the reasonability of premium levels; and any restrictions that may exist to the implementation of the programme through the captive, for example long term agreements with insurers and other contractual constraints, such as insuring requirements under the trust deed for debenture stock.

7.4.5 Spread of Risk

The study should include a detailed analysis of the portfolio of exposures. The number of independent units, their location and value has to be recorded. Particular attention has to be paid to potential exposures to large individual losses or accumulations from one event or in one year. These points are also of significance for the reinsurance costs and underwriting experience of the captive.

7.4.6. Premium Volume

When underwriting cover the captive will be seeking to achieve or reconcile the twin objectives of profitability and security. To this end the study will be required to analyse the relationship between the volume of premium available for each class of risk, the overall exposure at both individual and aggregate levels and the spread of risk within the portfolio, in order to ensure that it is sufficient to meet both the costs of reinsurance and retained losses. The profitability of the captive is dependent upon its underwriting experience, cash flow and reinsurance costs. Underwriting profitability is a function of a low claims history which in turn may be attributed to good loss control performance. These factors also influence reinsurance costs, as to obtain the highest level of cover for the lowest cost without sacrifice to quality of service it is necessary to demonstrate to the reinsurer that the premium that will be received is adequate to protect it against serious exposure. The strongest argument for this is to refer to a low loss frequency and loss potential. This also applies to the purchase of stop loss cover, where to ensure that the cost of cover is not too expensive, the reinsurer has to be reassured that the probability of the cover being invoked is remote.

The security or the protection of the captive fund against exhaustion is a function of the reinsurance cover purchased and the premium retained to fund the self-insured risks balanced against this exposure. Over-expenditure on reinsurance cover can deplete the ability of the captive to fund the retained risks, while on the other hand large uncovered losses can bankrupt the captive. A balance has to be struck between these elements.

7.4.7 Reinsurance

The basis upon which reinsurance can be arranged has to be examined. Reinsurance is available to protect against individual losses arising from a single event and accumulations of losses, whether arising from a single event or from a number of events within a year. Cover is arranged on one of three bases – surplus, quota share, or excess of loss. The pros and cons of each basis should be covered in the report. These will be dealt with at greater length in the next chapter.

Accumulations of loss from a single event are covered by excess of loss per risk reinsurance and accumulations of loss from a number of events are covered by stop loss reinsurance.

Reinsurance cover is rated on an experience basis so that its cost is related to the profitability to the reinsurer of the underlying account. This in turn is based on the loss history, the spread of risk and the values at risk as expressed by their EMLs in the captive's portfolio.

7.4.8 Cash Flow

The delay between receipt of premium and settlement of claims affords the captive the opportunity of generating investment income. The potential income varies according to the class of business but investment income can be realised even from short tail business. Crucial to these opportunities is the timing of the various cash flows, such as the receipt of premium following the issues of the cover, the payment of reinsurance premiums, settlement of claims, and reinsurance recoveries. Reinsurers tend to work on a regular account basis which means that the timing of these cash flows should be known in advance. Delays in the receipt of premium can vary considerably from country to country and thus significantly affect the ability to generate investment income. Countries where long delays are experienced should be noted perhaps with a view to excluding short tail business from coverage by the captive.

Given that substantial funds will be under the management of the captive, the investment policy has to be determined bearing in mind the need to maintain sufficient liquidity, to provide protection against the effects of inflation, to make settlements in foreign currencies, and to optimise the return from the fund given these constraints. Whether the funds are to be managed in-house, perhaps by the parent's treasury department, or externally by investment managers will also have to be decided.

Whatever policy is decided the cash flow position of the captive and the income arising from investment activities will have to be incorporated in an evaluation of the performance of the captive. The effect of delays in payment will also have to be included in analyses of alternative financing techniques such as conventional insurance in order that comparisons can be drawn.

7.4.9 Servicing Needs

The needs of the captive for both technical services such as risk control surveys and claims handling and other services such as fronting facilities have to be identified and costed. If fronting facilities are required, the capability of the insurers which currently handle the parent's insurances, or would be expected to become involved in a captive programme to provide these services, will have to be assessed to ensure they meet the needs of the programme.

7.4.10 Location

The first choice is between domestic and offshore. If it is decided to locate offshore there is a wide number of locations to choose from, not all of which would be suitable to a particular captive. The prospective locations for the situation of the captive are usually appraised on the following criteria:

- **Convenience:** this is of importance as most locations require the board meeting of the captive to be held where it is domiciled. Of necessity therefore the captive has to be within reasonable travelling time and transport facilities have to be regular, reliable and available at reasonable cost.

- **Communications:** the location has to be well-served in respect of telephone, telex and other communications facilities at reasonable cost in view of the necessity of the rapid transfer of information.

- **Insurance company legislation:** this often has an important bearing on the decision regarding location, as the legislation in many of the domestic locations with respect to capitalisation, solvency and reporting requirements impose costs and other constraints which render all but the largest of insurance subsidiaries unviable. Offshore centres actively seek to encourage captive formation through less rigorous requirements for the establishment and operation of the captive. The more relaxed regime leads to lower costs of establishment and operation, and speedier processing of applications.

- **Taxation:** the rate ruling in the prospective location will also be of interest to the captive parent as lower rates facilitate the quicker build up of risk bearing capacity, and defer tax liabilities at higher rates in the domicile of the parent if such a deferment can be achieved. In some locations the effect of double tax treaties needs to be considered.

- **Management companies and other services:** attention should also be paid to the infrastructure required for the operation of an insurance company, namely the existence, range, cost and competence of relevant expertise such as technical, accounting, legal, banking and other services.

- **Political stability of the location:** this point is self-explanatory and has to be raised because of the identity of some captive locations. Regardless of the position at the time of the study it is probably advisable that a contingency plan be prepared in the event of threats to sequestrate assets.

7.4.11 Overall Captive Exposure

An integrated captive programme involving a number of classes of risk needs to take the overall exposure of the financial resources of the insurance subsidiary into account. This process would include identifying exposures where a single event could lead to losses being retained under a number of different classes of cover, and taking account of these combined losses on the financial viability of the company. Likewise the outcome of poor loss experience resulting in a higher than expected number of events of high severity should also be tested.

It is unlikely that cover will be available to provide adequate protection across the board at an economic rate. If there is a risk of serious exposure from the combined risks then perhaps lower levels of retention on individual classes of risk should be considered. Alternatively, where classes are closely linked as in the case of fire and consequential loss, then the introduction of combined retention limits should be investigated.

The study should include a range of charts with performance projections for a minimum of five years, showing the effect of claims costs, reinsurances, fronting fees, management, and set-up costs. Table 7.3 gives an example for a captive in its first year of operation.

In summary, the purpose of the feasibility study is to determine whether it will meet its stated objectives, to identify how these objectives will be achieved, and to examine the implications for the viability of the captive.

Greene and Serbein in *Risk Management: Text and Cases* summarise the main features of a study as:

- the statement of the objectives;
- analyses of:
  - the current and projected exposures of the parent company according to source of loss;
  - current risk management costs;
  - captive set-up costs;
  - cash flow advantages and investment income;
  - alternative risk financing techniques, deductible and retention levels, reinsurance arrangements and their integration;
  - the arrangements for and costs of fronting facilities;
- description of:
  - the manner in which losses, loss evaluation, claims management and control will be handled;
  - the mechanics of the establishment and operation of the captive – its domicile, tax status, bylaws, incorporation, procedure, minimum capitalisation, officers, banking facilities, solicitors, accounting and other services;
- summary and final recommendations including standards of acceptable performance once the captive is established.

Table 7.3 – EXAMPLE OF THE DEVELOPMENT OF A CAPTIVE IN ITS FIRST YEAR OF OPERATION

a.	Premium to fronting insurer	£1,000,000
b.	Insurer's retention 10%	100,000
c.	Premium to captive	900,000
	Fronting fees 10%	90,000
		810,000
	Reinsurance cost net of commission	500,000
		310,000
	Management fees	30,000
		£280,000

Loss exposure £100,000 per loss
$300,000 stop loss

Year 1
Best position surplus £280,000 plus investment income.
Worst position deficit £20,000 plus loss of investment income on capital used to pay claims.
Capital at 50% solvency would be £155,000 which would reduce to £135,000.

SOURCE: P Bawcutt, *Captive Insurance Companies: Establishment, operation and management* 4th ed p 83. Witherby & Co Ltd London 1997

8

CAPTIVES (2)
OPERATION AND MANAGEMENT

8.1 INTRODUCTION

As may be gathered from the depth of information required of the feasibility study, the establishment of a captive is not a matter to be taken lightly. There are a number of operational issues that have to be addressed and understood in order to ensure its successful operation and practical requirements that have to be met. We shall turn our attention to these areas in more detail in this chapter, in particular:

(i)   the tax position of UK parented captives;

(ii) fronting facilities;

(iii) underwriting policy;

(iv) reinsurance facilities;

(v) selection of managers;

(vi) management responsibilities.

8.2 THE TAX POSITION OF CAPTIVES

In the previous chapter, it was established that a captive could be an effective and strategically beneficial mechanism for centrally financing retained risk. However, there are some important tax issues that need to be considered.

The majority of the world's most mature captive insurance domiciles have advantageous local corporation tax structures. However, for UK parented captives, Controlled Foreign Companies (CFC) legislation was introduced in 1984, and has been updated several times since, which reduces the tax benefits available significantly.

Chronologically, the following issues have affected the potential tax-efficiency of a UK parented captive:

- the 1984 Finance Act first introduced CFC legislation to the United Kingdom. A number of Exemptions, detailed later in this chapter, were available, however the vast majority of UK parented captives adopted the Acceptable Distribution Exemption, requiring 50% of the captive's profits to be repatriated to the UK as a dividend, whereupon they were subject to Corporation tax.

- the introduction of Insurance Premium Tax in July 1994 at the rate of 2.5% of gross premiums. This was subsequently increased to 4%, and subsequently 5%.

- in November 1995, the required dividend to meet the Acceptable Distribution Exemption increased from 50% to 90%.

- the introduction of Transfer Pricing Regulations in 1999 formally restricted the amount captives could charge as premiums.

- having changed the basis of calculating profits for the purpose of dividend distributions to 'UK chargeable profits', the introduction of General Insurance Reserve Discounting requirements, under Section 107 of the Finance Act 2000, further increased the potential UK tax liability. It was previously perceived that insurance companies had an unfair advantage over non-insurance entities in that they did not have to discount provisions to their net present value.

- changes to the Exempt Activities Exemption from CFC legislation introduced in Chancellor Gordon Brown's pre-Budget speech on 27th November 2002. One of the fundamental criteria to satisfy this Exemption was changed from a minimum of 50% unrelated gross trading receipts to a minimum of 50% unrelated gross trading receipts from parties resident outside of the United Kingdom.

The cumulative effect of the above has resulted in Balance Sheet risk retention being more cost-effective from a purely financial viewpoint in many cases than captive risk retention. However, for reasons described previously a captive remains a strategically important mechanism for risk retention. These strategic benefits frequently outweigh any financial burden represented by a captive.

8.2.1 Allowable Expense

To qualify as an allowable expense, any item must be incurred wholly and exclusively in the course of the company's business or trade. In order for premium paid to a captive to qualify, the parent must demonstrate that an effective transfer of risk has taken place.

The captive must therefore be adequately capitalised and able to bear the risk transferred from its own resources, including potential reinsurance recoveries.

Since payments by any insurer in respect of the settlement of claims are usually treated as chargeable income, the tax deductibility of the premium paid to the captive merely allows the parent to defer rather than avoid the tax charge on the income used to pay it, since the funds will ultimately be returned to the parent in settlement of claims. The principal benefit therefore is one of potential deferral rather than avoidance.

8.2.2 Residency

The residency of a company for UK tax purposes is determined not by its place of incorporation but where its central management and control actually reside. Normally this is regarded as being where the highest level of control of the business is exercised, for example where the board of directors meet and take decisions. This is frequently referred to as the 'Mind and Management' issue.

To ensure that non-UK residential status is maintained the management of the captive should ensure that:

- all general meetings of the company and directors meetings are held outside the UK;

- no instructions, orders or directives are passed from the UK concerning the running of the captive;

- the majority of the directors of the captive reside overseas, preferably in the location of the captive.

8.2.3 Controlled Foreign Companies

In the United Kingdom, and Europe generally, corporate taxation is primarily based upon residency. UK based companies are subject to tax on their individual profits, before consolidation of their subsidiaries' accounts.

The starting point for UK taxation of overseas subsidiaries is therefore that profits are taxable only when remitted to the UK as a dividend. This position is open to abuse and the UK government has introduced a raft of anti-avoidance legislation, under the title of Controlled Foreign Companies (CFC) legislation, the purpose of which is to remove the tax benefits for parents of subsidiaries which have been established totally or primarily for tax purposes. The effect of the legislation is to impute the profits of the CFC into the tax calculation of its parent.

In simplistic terms, a company resident outside the UK falls within the scope of this legislation when:

- it is effectively controlled by UK corporate entities; or

- more than 40% of its shares are held by a UK entity or related entities (although 'ownership' of more than 25% of the company's assets by a UK entity at the time of a theoretical liquidation date can be sufficient to be deemed a CFC); and

- it is subject to and pays corporate tax at a rate of less than 75% of the UK rate on its profits, calculated on a UK basis.

A UK parented captive therefore falls within CFC legislation if it is domiciled in a low tax area such as Guernsey or the Isle of Man. However, there are a number of exemptions from the CFC rules:

- **Motives Test:** the purpose of the captive is not to avoid UK tax and no UK tax is avoided. This is a very subjective test, which few captives have passed.

- **Exempt Activities Test:** the captive represents a standalone business and at least 50% of its net premium is derived from non-UK sources not related to its parent.

- **De Minimis Test:** the captive's profit (calculated on a UK basis) is less than £50,000.

- **Acceptable Distribution Test (ADT):** at least 90% of the captive's profit (calculated on a UK basis) is distributed as a dividend within 18 months of its financial year-end.

- **Excluded Countries:** a company in any of the countries on this list does not fall under the auspices of UK CFC. Under the Excluded Countries provision, the CFC must be both resident in and carrying on business in that country.

- **Public Quotation:** the public must hold shares carrying at least 35% of the voting rights of the CFC. The shares must not be preference shares and must be quoted on the exchange official list.

It should be noted that CFC tests and exemptions apply separately for each financial period and therefore a captive's status under CFC legislation is not fixed in perpetuity and may vary from year to year.

Whilst the above represents the position with regard to wholly-owned captives, the position with regard to cells in PCCs is less clear. Some observers have commented that, provided that the core of the PCC is owned by a non-UK entity, the profits arising in individual cells would only be subject to UK corporation tax when remitted to the UK as a dividend. One would assume, however, that if the assets attributable to any one cell at a theoretical liquidation date exceeded 25% of the entire PCC's assets, then it may be treated as a CFC.

8.2.4 Trading in or with the UK

A company which is not resident in the UK for tax purposes may nevertheless incur a liability to UK tax if it is found to be trading 'in' as opposed to 'with' the UK via a branch or agency. In this context, the relationship between the parent's insurance department, insurance manager or insurance broker and the captive may be vulnerable, and it is vital that such UK persons do not usurp the responsibilities of the captive's directors and offshore managers with regard to the acceptance of risks, settlement of claims, administration of funds, and so on.

8.2.5 Note of Caution

Whilst taxation is an important issue to most captive owners it should not dominate the feasibility issues. Taxation is a complex area and the risk manager should always seek external advice. Rules change frequently and the risk manager should secure professional advice on a regular basis, co-operating with other officials within the organisation in order to ensure a full and dynamic understanding is achieved.

8.3 FRONTING FACILITIES

In the last chapter we noted that a captive could be unable to issue policies direct to the insured. The reasons for this would include:

- non-admitted (unauthorised) insurers are prohibited from operating in the local market;

- compulsory insurances have to be written by locally admitted (authorised) insurers;

- commercial and political considerations may preclude the use of a captive when there is a local alternative available, for example in the case of a government contract; and

- the logistical problems for a multinational of establishing an insurance presence in the areas in which it is operating each with different legislation, reserve requirements, exchange control regulations and currencies.

In these circumstances a locally authorised insurer is appointed to insure the risks of the local company which will then be reinsured out to the captive. This arrangement can operate in all locations except those where there is a state monopoly over reinsurance. The risks will then be left in the local market and/or their own reinsurance programmes.

The fronting insurer usually provides the full range of insurance services such as:

- policy issue;

- claims handling;

- claims settlement;

- accounting;

- engineering services;

- loss control services.

8.3.1 Fronting Arrangements

Typically the fronting arrangement will involve the local insurer wholly underwriting the risk and then reinsuring the vast majority or all of it with the captive. A fronting fee is retained by the local insurer to cater for the costs incurred by it.

Additionally, the captive may have to satisfy the fronting insurer with regard to its own reinsurance arrangements. The assurances which may be sought include Letters of Credit, Escrow accounts, guarantees or indemnities from the parent company, or 'cut through' clauses in the fronting agreement to allow the insurer direct access to the reinsurers should the captive get into financial difficulty.

It is recommended that, wherever possible, the services of an international insurer be engaged to provide these fronting services because of its experience, local knowledge, resources and the ability to remit premiums more quickly to the captive than may be possible for a local insurer. Furthermore, in order to secure fronting services at the optimal cost, it is beneficial for the fronting insurer to also be the primary external risk carrier – for example as reinsurer of the captive.

However it is generally unwise to have more than three insurers operating in this capacity. If one or more of these insurers also handles other parts of the parent's programme of insurances so much the better, as this will allow a greater measure of co-ordination of the global programme. There may still be occasions when the use of a local admitted insurer is the most appropriate course of action.

The arrangement of fronting facilities remains a complex business, especially for the multinational corporation. Even with the services of an international insurer, many problems continue, as in some cases deposits with the direct insurer in respect of premium, and losses or delays in the remittance of premium as a result of accounting delays in the local market or exchange control regulations, may be unavoidable.

In the current environment it is quite difficult to secure fronting services at relatively low cost. The requirement for LOCs is also a sensitive issue.

8.4 UNDERWRITING

The underwriting policy is crucial as sufficient income has to be generated by the captive to meet the operating costs normally encountered by any insurance company, namely claims, reinsurance premiums, administration expenses, brokerage and commissions paid for business introduced, and fees paid for services purchased, plus a contribution to profits if the captive's objective is to operate as a profit generating entity for the parent.

8.4.1 Underwriting Policy

At the outset therefore the captive will have to decide the basis of the rating system on which risks will be underwritten. The premium structure can be based on one of the following systems:

(i) direct insurance market rates;

(ii) reinsurance market; or

(iii) a system devised by the captive itself.

8.4.1.1 Direct Insurance Market Rates

In the direct market the majority of risks are rated either according to class or experience. In class rating the rate for a class of exposure – material damage, business interruption, etc – is developed from the collective loss experience of an industry, trade or profession. The insurer collects data from a wide range of risks for a particular exposure – fire damage to warehouses for example. The average loss from each exposure is first calculated and thereafter the average loss for the group. This figure is then divided by a denominator common to all the other exposures to give the rate. In the above example this would be the area occupied by the warehouse – square feet or metres. The resultant rate can then be applied to any similar risk.

Experience rating is based on the loss experience of the individual insured and is usually only suitable for high frequency, low severity risks. Employer's liability and motor are the most common classes of business where this method is used.

Where there is a lack of data of sufficient quality because of a new or unknown risk, underwriters have to make a subjective assessment and therefore rating of the risks being underwritten. This point may be of some significance to the captive as it occasionally may be required to provide cover for such risks.

If market rates are used and the parent's loss experience is favourable, the captive will be able to make an underwriting profit. In addition it will also benefit from the investment income.

Alternatively a discount on market rates could be offered to the parent. This may be a particularly appropriate strategy to encourage the use of the captive, if the parent has a decentralised management structure. The group companies then benefit directly through lower premium cost and indirectly through the investment income accrued by the captive.

8.4.1.2 Reinsurance Market Rates

Using reinsurance market rates as a basis for the premium structure is in effect a cost plus strategy. The reinsurance costs plus a loading sufficient to finance the risk retained by the captive are charged to the parent. Since reinsurance rates are more closely tied to loss experience than those in the direct markets, improvements in loss experience will be automatically reflected in reinsurance premium costs. So the parent benefits directly through reduced premium expenditure while the captive continues to have access to investment income.

8.4.1.3 Tailored System

If the captive wishes to evolve its own rating system, this places certain requirements on the quality and scope of the data to which it has access. Insurers of course are in an advantageous position in this respect, as their portfolio of policies will be substantially larger.

This route therefore carries the risk that, due to inadequacy of available data, the premium charged will prove insufficient to meet expenses. This may put an unnecessary burden on capital employed in the captive, rather than ongoing premium contributions from the business units using the service provided by the captive.

8.4.2 Premium Allocation

Whatever the method chosen, the premium structure may also be expected to reflect the underwriting experience of the various subsidiaries, divisions, units of operation throughout the group. This however is a further level of sophistication, and the extent to which it is developed beyond even a simple premium allocation system depends on the benefits that will accrue in terms of commitment to risk management, balanced against the costs of developing such a system.

8.5 REINSURANCE

An important reason for forming a captive may be the access this gives the parent to reinsurance markets. The principal benefits of such access are:

- lower costs;

- greater flexibility of the market, both in the forms of protection available and the response to new risks;

- fewer legislative controls.

Generally, as there will be more markets available to a captive insurer than a non-insurance corporate entity, there will be greater competition leading to lower premiums for the parent's risk. In recent years this 'theory' has been called into question.

8.5.1 The Reinsurance Market

The reinsurance market is a wholesale market for insurance and as in all markets is made up of buyers and sellers. The sellers ('reinsurers') are reinsurance companies, Lloyds underwriting syndicates and direct insurance companies. The buyers ('cedants') are direct insurers, underwriting agencies, Lloyd's syndicates and other reinsurers. Reinsurance can be arranged either on a direct basis between the reinsurer and cedant or through an intermediary – the reinsurance broker.

The market exists to allow risks which are too large for a single insurer to be shared by a number of others or as a means of further spreading risk. As a wholesale market it is usually only open to participants from the insurance industry. It is a highly developed and professional market and has developed its own way of doing business. As a result, involvement with reinsurance markets requires technical expertise and understanding of the market. The services of a specialist such as a reinsurance broker are therefore normally required by captives wishing to purchase protection.

8.5.2 Reinsurance Contracts

A contract for reinsurance can be drawn up on either a facultative or treaty basis. Facultative reinsurance is a tailored or 'one-off' arrangement with a separate contract for each risk reinsured. Its use is therefore usually reserved for the reinsurance of larger, specialist or 'awkward' risks. Treaty reinsurance on the other hand is an 'off the peg' package written in advance for risks which as yet are unknown but conform to the terms of the contract, and thus provides a form of blanket cover. New exposures do not require a separate treaty but are added to the treaty or 'declared'. As these declarations are made further premium is required from the cedant.

Because of the limited amount of shareholders' funds available to meet claims in a typical captive, it is imperative that its exposures are limited in some form, both to individual losses and to the cumulative effect of the frequency of losses.

Where a captive has not assumed its risk as a net reinsurance arrangement, with its each and every loss and aggregate exposures limited, it may be necessary for its exposures to be protected by specific reinsurance protection. Schematics of the two most common structures of captive participation are shown in Figure 8.1:

Fig 8.1

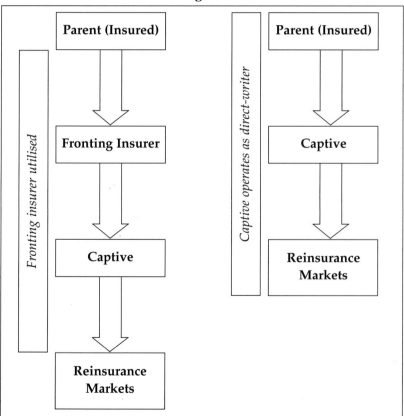

Schematics of the two most Common Structures of Captive Participation

Reinsurance can be arranged on a treaty or facultative basis.

Treaty reinsurance is usually arranged to cover a specific class of risk. The treaty stipulates the minimum retention level and the maximum capacity accepted by the reinsurer. Cover is automatically available for the risks mentioned in the contract and both the cedant and reinsurer are obliged to use the facility and accept the risks respectively.

Treaty reinsurance is commonly used by the commercial insurance markets, that do not know at any given time exactly what risks will be underwritten during the course of the following year.

Captives generally arrange their reinsurance in the direct insurance marketplace (albeit the contracts are structured as a reinsurance rather than insurance) or the specialist facultative markets. In facultative reinsurance the contract is written to cover a particular risk, with the reinsurer being free to accept or reject the risk. Once accepted it can charge rates or impose conditions as appropriate to the risk. In many respects the facultative market operates in exactly the same manner as the direct insurance markets as far as captives are concerned.

On occasion, a captive may be expected to offer coverage to its parent for risks that the conventional commercial insurance market may not be willing to cater for. The alternative risk financing market has grown significantly during the 1990s, with many captives seeking protection in non-conventional arrangements.

The most common forms of non-conventional protection are finite reinsurance and contingent capital programmes, which are the subject of greater attention in Chapter 11.

8.5.3 Forms of Reinsurance

Facultative or treaty reinsurance can be either proportional or non-proportional in form. In proportional reinsurance the cedant and the reinsurer share the gross premium and losses in agreed proportions. Non-proportional reinsurance involves the cedant bearing a pre-determined sum, with losses in excess of this being passed on to the reinsurer. The main forms of proportional and non-proportional reinsurance are summarised in Figure 8.2.

Fig 8.2

CONTRACT		FORM OF REINSURANCE
		• Quota share
		• Surplus
		• Pools
FACULTATIVE OR TREATY		
		• Excess of Loss (Risk bases)
		• Excess of Loss (per occurrence)

		• Stop Loss
		  − aggregate excess
		  − excess of loss ratio

Proportional		Non-proportional

Proportional and Non-proportional Reinsurance

8.5.3.1 Proportional Reinsurance

Quota share

Under this arrangement the cedant is obliged to cede a fixed proportion of each risk underwritten to the reinsurer, with premiums being shared in the same proportion. This obligation means that a cedant cannot select which exposures to select or retain. Thus potentially profitable exposures are also ceded to the reinsurer. The benefit to the cedant is a stabilisation of loss experience as the loss ratio remains unchanged.

For example if an insurer has agreed a 75% quota share treaty with a gross capacity of £1,000,000 with a reinsurer, then given a cedant retention level of £250,000 the losses would be shared as shown in Table 8.1.

Table 8.1

| Loss | Financed by | |
| | Cedant | Reinsurer |
£	£	£
50,000	12,500	37,500
250,000	62,500	187,500
600,000	150,000	450,000
1,000,000	250,000	750,000

The reinsurer and the cedant share the losses on a 75:25 ratio to a maximum of £1,000,000. Losses in excess of this level are not subject to the agreement and will have to be financed either by the cedant or by means of another layer of reinsurance.

Surplus

Under a surplus agreement the proportion in which losses are shared between the cedant and reinsurer is dependent on the retention level of the cedant.

The capacity of the reinsurer is measured in 'lines', one of which is equal to the cedant's retention. Thus a reinsurer can accept a multiple of the retention level or line subject to an agreed limit. For example if the cedant's retention is £50,000 and the gross capacity required is £250,000, then a five-line treaty would be required. The programme would operate as shown as Table 8.2

Table 8.2

| Sum Insured | Cedant's Retention | Reinsurer's Share | Share (%) |
£	£	£	
10,000	10,000	–	–
80,000	50,000	30,000	37.5
300,000	50,000	250,000	83.3

In contrast to quota share, the cedant can retain more of its own business by selecting an appropriate level of retention. The amount ceded can therefore be reduced with a corresponding saving in premium. However, these savings must be offset against increased administration requirements as the reinsurer will require regular reports of premiums received and losses incurred.

Pools

These are formed by companies agreeing to underwrite hazardous risks such as nuclear risks and certain marine and aviation risks, with each participating carrying an agreed portion of all business in the pool. Any risk accepted by a member of the pool is then wholly reinsured into the pool.

8.5.3.2 Non-proportional

Non-proportional business is distinguished from proportional business in the manner in which losses are shared and the premium set.

Excess of loss (Risk Basis)

Reinsurance on this basis is effected to cover losses arising from a single occurrence for a specific risk or class of business. The purpose of it is to protect the cedant's resources and enable it to increase its loss-bearing capacity.

It operates in a manner similar to the deductible arrangement in conventional insurance in that the cedant bears a fixed amount of each and every loss. If a loss exceeds this pre-determined level the reinsurer funds the balance of the claim. The cedant in fact, under the terms of the contract, is liable for the whole amount of the loss, and then claims subsequent to the loss against the reinsurer for sums in excess of the retention level.

It is normal for the reinsurer to limit its exposure by setting a maximum level of liability and limiting the number of times that cover can be reinstated during the period. The total cover required however may be greater than that which a single reinsurer is willing to bear. In these cases it is necessary to arrange the cover in different layers with one or more reinsurers underwriting the various layers.

For example, if the maximum exposure is estimated to be £7,000,000, the reinsurance programme could be arranged in the layers shown in Table 8. 3.

Table 8.3

Layer	Amount £	Reinsured by	Total £
Retained by cedant	500,000	–	500,000
1st excess of loss	2,500,000	ReA Ltd (50%) ReB Ltd (25%) ReC Ltd (25%)	3,000,000
2nd excess of loss	2,500,000	ReA Ltd (50%) ReB Ltd (25%) ReD Ltd (25%)	5,500,000
3rd excess of loss	1,500,000	Cedant	7,000,000

Excess of loss per occurrence

This differs from the previous form in that cover is extended to embrace a number of losses arising from the same event, for example storm or explosion. The purpose of the cover is to protect a cedant against a build-up of retained losses due to multiple claims arising from a single event.

Cover is available for an accumulation of losses either:

- within a single class of exposure; or

- across a number of distinct classes of exposure.

The former is referred to as 'catastrophe' reinsurance and the latter as 'umbrella' or 'clash' reinsurance.

The cover is arranged on terms which are similar to the excess of loss basis, namely there is a predetermined retention level to be borne by the cedant; losses in excess of the retention level are borne by the reinsurer. The cedant is liable for the whole of the loss and subsequently recovers from the reinsurer. The reinsurance cover can be layered as illustrated above.

Stop loss cover

This can be arranged on the basis of either aggregate excess of loss or excess of loss ratio. Its function is to protect a cedant against the effects of an aggregation of retained losses from a single class of business over a specified period of time – normally a year. These retentions can arise from either or both the retained and other loss layers assumed by the cedant. The stop loss protects the cedant's loss experience by limiting its annual retention to a predetermined level. It is of particular value in the earlier years of the cedant, although the additional protection has to be balanced against the reduced premium available to fund net retentions and conform to statutory solvency requirements. The levels can be raised or removed as the fund matures.

(i) In aggregate excess of loss the reinsurer stipulates in its terms of cover the amount in the aggregate that it is prepared to cover. For example if a cedant has a £50,000 retention, the reinsurer could offer cover for losses in excess of £150,000 each claim and in the aggregate per annum, in which case the retained losses of the cedant will be confined to £150,000 per annum.

If the reinsurer offers unlimited cover the cedant will have no further exposure. This however can emerge if the reinsurer limits its liability, in which case the cedant would be exposed to losses in excess of the reinsured layer. To illustrate, if in the above example the reinsurer limits its liability to £750,000 each claim and in the aggregate per annum (in excess of £150,000 each claim and in the aggregate per annum), the cedant will be covered for annual aggregate losses from £150,000 to £900,000. Thereafter it is exposed for annual aggregate losses in excess of this limit.

(ii) The excess of loss ratio relates to the point at which the reinsurance is activated to the net premium paid by the cedant. Net premium is used to calculate the claims ratio as follows:

$$\frac{\text{Net claims (claims less reinsurance recoveries)}}{\text{Net premium (premium less reinsurance costs)}} \; x \;\; 100$$

If, for example, a limit of 75% is set for this ratio then losses which take the ratio beyond this level are borne by the reinsurer. Hence if net premium income is £2,000,000 the cedant's retention will be £1,500,000.

The reinsurer may agree to take the next 35% of losses in excess of the cedant's retention but limit its liability to 90% of any losses within this layer. The reinsurer thus protects its position by limiting its liability to a percentage of a specific loss layer.

The following illustrations demonstrate the excess of loss ratio in operation and the effect of reinsurance on the claims ratio of the cedant.

Cedant's retention   =   75%

Net premium income =   £2,000,000

Reinsurance   =   90% of losses in excess of 75% up to 110% of net premium income

Table 8.4 – SIZE OF LOSS £1,900,000

Layer	Without reinsurance Financed by Cedant	Claims ratio	With reinsurance Financed by Cedant	Reinsurer	Claims ratio
£	£	%	£	£	%
1,500,000	1,500,000	75	1,500,000	–	75
400,000	400,000	100	40,000	360,000	77

Table 8.5 – SIZE OF LOSS = £2,300,000

Layer	Without reinsurance Financed by Cedant	Claims ratio	With reinsurance Financed by Cedant	Reinsurer	Claims ratio
£	£	%	£	£	%
1,500,000	1,500,000	75	1,500,000	–	75
700,000	700,000	110	70,000	630,000	78
100,000	100,000	120	100,000	–	83

Thus the claims ratio of the cedant has been materially improved by the use of reinsurance facilities.

8.5.3.3 Dealing with the Market

As we have already observed, dealing with the reinsurance market requires specialist assistance for both technical expertise and market knowledge. Expertise is required for the preparation and presentation of the risk to the market and the subsequent negotiations with it. Knowledge of the market and in particular the solvency and security of reinsurers is vital, as the financial viability of the captive rests on the solvency of its reinsurers. Finally, the services of a reputable and established reinsurance broker enhances the position of the insured in its presentation to and subsequent dealings with the market.

A number of points of general significance have to be borne in mind when dealing with the reinsurance market:

- avoid dependence upon a single reinsurer. This spreads risk in the market;

- deal with awkward/special/unusual risks on a facultative rather than a treaty basis;

- ensure the solvency of reinsurers, especially for long tail exposures;

- recognise the importance placed by the reinsurance market upon loss control and its effect on loss experience;

- ensure accurate valuation of EMLs since these form the bases for excess loss and stop loss cover;

- regularly update covers, limits, and sums insured;

- ensure the timely remittance of premiums from the parent in order to protect the captive's cash flow. Reinsurance premiums normally are settled either quarterly or half-yearly. There are occasions, however, when there may be delays in the remittance of funds due to local reserving requirements or exchange control regulations.

8.5.4 Conclusion

The captive's relationship with the reinsurance market should be viewed as a long term one, in which case the chief concern should be for quality of service and support from the market rather than the lowest price. The reinsurance market is a volatile place, but this can be mitigated through good long-standing relationships with underwriters which yield a return in the long run. Finally, since a good loss record is the best recommendation to the reinsurance market, this brings us back to the influence of the risk management practice of the parent upon the financial viability of the captive.

8.6 OPERATIONAL AND ADMINISTRATIVE REQUIREMENTS

The operations of a captive insurance company mean that it has to draw upon a wide range of services to fulfil its role. These services would have to include the following:

- legal advice;
- underwriting expertise;
- preparation of accounts;
- claims handling activities;
- investment management.

Legal advice

Legal advice may be required initially to incorporate the company and thereafter on an ad-hoc basis to provide specific advice, for example on complex claims issues.

Underwriting expertise

The captive must have knowledge of market practice in both the direct and reinsurance markets as well as expertise in relation to the rating of risks.

Furthermore, the expertise must encompass documentary requirements. All insurance contracts are evidenced by policy documentation, and a captive is no different. Furthermore, expertise will be required to check reinsurance policy terms, to ensure that the captive is adequately protected, and that claims against the captive do not inadvertently fall into any differences in the cover afforded by it and its reinsurance protection.

Preparation of accounts

Expertise must exist to meet the specialised needs of insurance accounting. This would include the separation of premium funds, charging of unearned premium, reserving for reported and incurred but not reported claims, distinguishing between free and technical reserves, and meeting auditing requirements.

The captive will be required to prepare management accounts, either monthly or quarterly dependent upon the parent's requirements, annual financial statements, budgets, and also tailored returns to meet the regulator's requirements.

Claims handling activities

The necessary skills in claims handling must also be available for the reporting, investigation, adjustment, negotiation, and settlement of claims under policies which have been issued either directly or through a fronting insurer; insurance recoveries; and the salvage of damaged property.

Investment management

Dependent on the financial size of the captive, the services of competent investment managers may be required to optimise the investment return whilst meeting statutory solvency requirements and maintaining adequate liquidity in the light of the business being written. This will involve the development of cash flow forecasts incorporating the timing and receipt of premium and investment income, and expenditure on claims and reinsurance premiums.

8.6.1 Administration

The regulations of most captive locations require that the company be incorporated in the location and have its registered office there. This means that the company must have premises, means of communication with the parent's and other locations, staff and local directors. These can be provided either in-house or by a specialised management company.

The persons responsible for the management of the captive must be 'fit and proper' persons and competent to carry out their responsibilities. In many domiciles, professional captive management companies are regulated entities themselves. The tasks which will be expected of the captive include:

- the issue of policy documents;
- the settlement of claims either direct or by delegation to a claims handling agent;
- the maintenance of accounts and the preparation of financial statements;
- the preparation and submission of statutory returns as required by the supervisory authorities; and
- the initiation and organisation of meetings of the Board and

general meetings of the company as necessary to manage the company, and also in accord with the regulatory requirements.

8.7 MANAGEMENT OF THE CAPTIVE

A captive can be managed either in-house or by a company specialising in their management. This is possible because the captive's primary role is as a risk financing vehicle for the parent. As such we have seen its main business consists in the collection of premium, the payment of claims, and the issue of policy documents – functions which can be delegated to an external body. Other services such as surveys, engineering, claims handling, etc can be purchased separately as we have already observed.

8.7.1 In-House Management

The cost of staffing an insurance subsidiary with the relevant professional personnel and secretarial support infers that there is sufficient premium volume and work to justify such expenditure. The view of this expenditure depends of course on the original objective as identified in the feasibility study. If the intention is to create a profit centre or eventually to expand into unrelated business then the employment of staff by the captive may be deemed to be necessary. Moreover in order to exploit the benefits of the offshore location the in-house operation will have to be situated there, separate from the parent company to comply with local regulations.

8.7.2 Management Company

For many companies, the economics of captive management would preclude the formation of a captive, as in the early part of its life there may be insufficient business to justify the appointment of staff. In these circumstances the management company can perform all the tasks required for a significantly lower cost and allow the captive to operate efficiently.

Management companies are not only used by new companies. They can offer expertise, experience and economies of scale through specialisation which will probably not be available to the parent company from its own resources. Furthermore they are located in all of the principal offshore locations.

There are a number of independent management companies and groups specialising solely in such activities, but for the most part they are subsidiaries of insurance brokers, underwriting agents, lawyers, accountants or banks.

8.7.3 Duties of Management Companies

The duties to be performed by the management company will be specified in the management agreement and are specific to the company and the parent. However, a good management company should be able to provide underwriting expertise, insurance accounting and company secretarial services, as well as facilities such as the registered office. In more detail this would infer the provision of the following services:

- underwriting
  - development and maintenance of suitable programmes of insurance to be accepted;
  - development and maintenance of suitable reinsurance programmes to be ceded or accepted;
  - drafting and issuing of policy wordings and of all other documentation;

- accounting
  - establishing loss and unearned premium reserves;
  - claims handling and settlement;
  - regular and comprehensive management reporting;
  - preparation of statutory accounts;
  - supervision of bank accounts and investments;
  - maintenance of accounting records;

- company secretarial services
  - the arrangement of company incorporation and insurance registration;
  - provision of registered office and boardroom facilities;
  - introduction to appropriately qualified local directors;
  - maintenance of all other corporate records;
  - preparation of insurance returns.

It will also be the responsibility of the management company to ensure that the regulatory requirements of the particular location are complied with in such matters as the solvency margin of the captive, admissibility of its assets, minimum reserve requirements, the frequency and location of meetings of the Board, and the expertise and domicile of the directors.

8.7.4 Appointment of the Management Company

When selecting the management company the parent should ensure that it can provide all of the services listed above and then be guided by the extent of its experience in the area, its standing with the insurance market, and reputation in the relevant captive location. Once appointed the performance of the managers should be reviewed regularly. Furthermore, the risk manager should assume an active role in its management, through contact with other companies operating in the same location and regular updates of changes in the markets and captive developments.

The management company should be appointed by means of a properly constituted legal document clearly delineating the functions, responsibilities and authority of the manager. It is important to establish the areas in which the manager requires the consent of the Board to operate. In general, the management agreement should cover the following matters:

- the powers available to the manager to carry out his duties, such as to issue policies, settle claims or maintain bank accounts;

- the reporting requirement to the parent with respect to premiums, claims and final accounts;

- responsibility for compliance with statutory requirements of the location – the submissions of documents, reporting requirements, etc;

- the policies of the captive with respect to (a) investments, and (b) the funding of claims and the reserving for outstanding claims;

- the position on errors and omissions of the managers;

- the remuneration of the managers. This is normally an annually agreed flat fee basis, although in larger cases may be on a time and expense basis.

9

INSURANCE (1)
ANALYSIS AND EVALUATION

9.1 INTRODUCTION

The prominence of insurance in many risk financing programmes demands a systematic approach to its purchase. Insurance is only an effective risk financing technique when the cover provided by the insurance contract matches the needs of the organisation. Adequate compensation in the event of loss is ensured and the organisation is able to continue with its operations.

The existence of cover for a particular event or peril should not be taken for granted. Policy terms and conditions have to be checked thoroughly. A methodical approach becomes all the more important when comparing covers written by competing insurers. The complexities of international insurances, where the purchaser also has to contend with the variations in the definitions of perils, necessitates a structured approach to the selection of insurance cover.

The tragic events of September 11th 2001 were a catalyst for a hardening insurance market. During the period 1980 to 2001 combined ratios for the insurance industry in general were in the order of 100% to 115%. According to the Insurance Information Institute, the gap between cumulative GDP and relative premium growth exceeded 50% from the base year of 1987. In recent years coupled with a declining stock market, underwriting on this basis clearly could not be sustained. Insurance costs are now a significant and material expense in many corporate budgets. The increase in and the absolute sums involved have brought insurance premiums to the attention of corporate finance directors. The financial criterion may be more concerned with the 'return' from such expenditure than the 'protection'.

The economic viability of insurance has therefore come under scrutiny. If scarce corporate resources are being allocated – and in increasing amounts – what is the return? Could these funds be used more effectively in another fashion? In other words the purchase of insurance is subjected to the same criteria as other major commitments of corporate revenues.

9.2 NATURE OF INSURANCE

Insurance is a mechanism for providing financial protection against specified contingencies such as death and loss or damage to property, and depends on the pooling or combination of the risks of two or more parties. Contributions are made by each insured to the fund in relation to the level of risk brought to the pool and the insurer undertakes to settle claims out of the pool as they arise.

Insurance therefore is a means of providing for the wide range of losses to which an organisation is subject. These are classified in Table 9.1.

Table 9.1

PROPERTY	Largely material damage.
LIABILITY	Damages paid to third parties in compensation for injury, death or loss of property arising from the actions of the organisation or its employees.
PERSONNEL	Loss suffered by the organisation arising out of the loss of a 'key person', or costs of employee benefits in excess of statutory minimum.
PECUNIARY	Arising out of monetary loss due to dishonesty of employees, customers or others, or business interruption loss costs.

Classification of Wide Ranging Possible Losses

The full range of exposures to which the organisation is subject should have been identified at the risk identification stage of the risk management process.

9.2.1 Risk Transfer

Insurance provides financial protection against loss by enabling the purchaser to transfer the risk of loss to the insurer upon the fulfilment of certain conditions. The key features of the insurance contract are:

- it is arranged in advance of the event and documented in writing in the insurance policy;

- the loss is transferred at the time of the incident;

- only the financial consequences of the loss are transferred;

- the insured still has to suffer the loss of buildings, plant or stock before the financial compensation is available.

Insurance is a contractual agreement, meaning that the availability of financial compensation depends on the terms of the cover. These are governed by the legal doctrines of insurance – utmost good faith, insurable interest, indemnity, proximate cause, subrogation and contribution.

For example, the principle of indemnity will affect the settlement figure, raising the issue of 'betterment' in a number of cases, and also the manner in which settlement is provided, such as repair or replacement rather than a monetary sum. From time to time the Courts may also rule on wording or terms, which may alter the complexion of the contract upon which the transfer of the risk is based.

If insurance is viewed as a contractual risk transfer, this inevitably raises questions as to whether cover will be available and in what form. Part of the analysis of insurance cover must therefore include an examination of the terms and conditions under which risk is transferred to ensure that this will be effective.

9.2.2 Risk Financing

The normal pattern of an insurance contract is that a premium is paid, after which claims occur and ultimately are settled.

Or put another way, the insured pays money to the insurer who then repays some, all, or more than the sum received upon the occurrence of an event or events stipulated in the cover. Always there is a time delay between payment of the premium and settlement of the claim. In some years less will be repaid than was received by the insurer, in others it will be the reverse; and it is likely that not all the funds will be repaid at the same time. The basic pattern is of cash paid out by the insured, followed by a delay, followed by cash received by the insured.

This is particularly noticeable at lower levels of loss where there is a pattern of low severity and high frequency. It is sometimes described as 'pound (or dollar) swapping' because the insured receives in settlement all of the premium that has been paid, less a proportion for the insurer's expenses and profit loadings. This has been acknowledged in recent years and insurers have subsequently been prepared to allow the insured to assume responsibility for payment of 'lower layer' losses, thus eliminating the disproportionate expenses associated with this layer of loss.

The principle also holds good for middle and upper layer losses, the major difference being the period over which the premium is collected to pay for the loss. The insurer must eventually recover all sums paid otherwise it will not be able to survive.

In essence insurance is a short-term risk transfer device. The cost of the loss is borne ultimately by the insured, not the insurer, as poor loss experience will lead to higher premiums, all other things being equal. Insurance therefore is a loss smoothing device requiring the organisation to fund its own losses in the long run, whilst providing protection against the financial disruption of a middle to large-scale loss in the short run.

If insurance is to be viewed in this light it has to be treated as another source of finance, and by the same token requires a different process of evaluation from that associated with risk transfer. The organisation will be interested to discover how it rates in comparison with other sources of finance. Thus analysis will concentrate on cash flows rather than contract terms, and the question will no longer be "is it covered?", but rather "given that it is covered, is it more or less expensive than alternative sources of finance?".

A significant distortion is, however, due to the fact that long term insurance contracts are extremely rare and it is almost impossible to build a partnership agreement when considering the lower layer risk financing approach.

9.2.3 Benefits of Insurance

Insurance bestows a number of practical benefits upon the buyer, which would include:

- indemnification against unexpected loss;

- reduction in uncertainty;

- release of funds for more productive use; and

- access to specialist risk management services provided by insurers.

9.2.3.1 Indemnity

Insurance represents a guaranteed source of funds when the availability of other sources may be restricted as a result of the loss. Lenders may be unwilling to advance funds to an organisation which has had its ability to repay curtailed by virtue of being deprived of some of its revenue earning capacity. In such circumstances a ready source of finance may be exactly what is required to minimise the effects of the loss on operations. Thus the ready availability of funds from the insurer will serve to mitigate the effects of the loss, as production or services are restored and revenue earning capacity replaced.

9.2.3.2 Reduction of Uncertainty

Uncertainty is reduced by the purchase of insurance in a number of ways:

- financing arrangements. Different loss layers have different financing requirements. What is appropriate for small regular losses is not suitable for those which are medium or large scale;

- timing of loss. Although severity and frequency of annual average losses can be predicted, this is rarely the case with the timing of losses;

- substitution of unknown costs with the known cost of the premium.

As risks are pooled an insurer has access to larger quantities of data than would be feasible for the individual insured. By virtue of the law of large numbers, predictability is enhanced thus reducing the overall level of risk. The individual unit benefits as provisions for unexpected losses in any year are now not only smaller but restricted to the premium.

9.2.3.3 Economic Benefit

This reduction in uncertainty is also of economic benefit. Funds which previously would have had to have been held in liquid form to meet unexpected losses can now be released for other uses yielding a higher return.

According to Williams and Heins in *Risk Management and Insurance,* "the reduction of uncertainty will encourage the accumulation of new capital because investors are less likely to hesitate; planning periods are lengthened, credit is more generally extended, and fewer resources are hoarded. The price structures are further improved by the fact that the insurers estimate of the expected for each insured is generally superior to that of the individual unit".

9.2.3.4 Specialist Risk Control Services

Many ancillary services which are provided by the insurer and included in the cost of the premium are valued by the insured because of the access to the experience and expertise of the insurer. If such services as fire, theft or liability surveys, loss adjusting or claims were not provided by the insurer, the insured would have to provide them either from within its own resources or from an outside source.

9.2.4 Criticisms of Insurance

The use of insurance as a risk financing tool is not without its problems. Insurance rarely provides full financial compensation for loss due to:

- delays in restoration to full productive use;
- delays in settlement arising out of:
  - difficulty in assessing the loss; or
  - dispute with the insurer;
- permanent loss of market share.

Cover is available for loss of earnings or additional costs due, incurred because of interruptions to production, but this does not last indefinitely nor does it compensate for loss of market share or damage to market standing.

There are a number of practical problems experienced by the insured, which can fall into one of three main areas:

(i) the insurance market;

(ii) the management of insurances;

(iii) the performance of insurers.

9.2.4.1 The Insurance Market

The chief concerns in this area are:

- lack of cover often in areas where it is most required, for example US products liability in recent years – this is now a major issue for many sectors;

- difficulties of comparing covers of competing insurers;

- the premium charged by the market does not reflect the loss experience of the buyer; and

- the threat of insurer bankruptcy. Recently the insurance market has seen many downgrades and negative watch recommendations by the rating agencies.

9.2.4.2 The Management of Insurances

The following problems have arisen in the management of insurances:

- uninsured losses due to failure:
    - to identify potential loss;
    - to arrange cover for new property acquired;
    - to conform to requirements of insuring arrangements;

- underinsurance;

- overinsurance due to:
    - exposures insured twice;
    - overlapping covers;
    - insurance of non-existent exposure;

- uneconomic insurances where for example there has been a failure to identify that a small deductible would yield substantial premium savings;

- failure to compare insurance prices or employ competitive bidding;

- insurance programmes not reviewed regularly or updated;

- adequate insurance and loss records not maintained;

- responsibility for insurance management not identified.

9.2.4.3 The Performance of Insurers

Buyer dissatisfaction with insurers is often directed at:

- poor quality of service;

- the cost of premiums relative to the company's own loss experience;

- the volatility of premium costs. Insurance is supposed to lead to the reduction of uncertainty. If however insurance market conditions lead to wide fluctuations in rates quoted, uncertainty is reintroduced.

9.3 THE POLICY DOCUMENT

We have seen that insurance is a contractual arrangement. The terms of the contract are recorded in the policy document issued by the insurer. Companies have developed standard policy wordings and structures for purposes of convenience, speed and accuracy. The wordings are carefully formulated to ensure that only the risk that the insurer intends to accept is actually transferred in the event of a loss. In certain parts of the UK market, specifically fire and marine, companies have adopted uniform policy wordings.

With the exception of this market, buyers of insurance will be faced with a range of policy wordings from competing insurers. The problem of appraising policy terms becomes more acute when arranging international coverages. However by virtue of the legal principles governing insurance, the nature of the demands of contract terms, and trade custom and practice, most policies do conform to a pattern.

For example the general form of fire policy in use in the UK is the scheduled policy. The different parts are arranged in a specific manner with the information relating to the individual contract detailed in a separate list.

Policies are generally arranged in the following sections:

1. The **declaration/recital/preamble** clause which details:

   - the name of the insured;
   - the premium;
   - the risk covered;

- the types and terms of the coverage;
- the policy limits (usually in the schedule/specification of the scheduled policy); and
- a declaration that the proposal form is the basis of the insurance contract and is incorporated in it.

2. The **attestation** clause stating what the insurer agrees to do.

3. The **operative** clause stating the specific events or perils insured against.

4. The **exclusions** clause, which in some forms of cover is required to specifically exclude certain perils such as property, sources of liability or locations.

5. **Conditions**

   (i) That have to be fulfilled before the insurer is liable:

   (a) *precedent to contract,* that is implied by law to apply to all insurance contracts;

   (b) *subsequent to contract,* that is requirements, such as advice of changes in exposure, to be fulfilled once the cover is in place;

   (c) *precedent to liability,* that is steps that the insured has to take subsequent to loss to ensure the transfer of liability to the insurer.

   (ii) The rights and obligations of the insured and insurer following a loss, which can be either general conditions which usually reinforce common law provisions relating to fraud, restriction of cover and so on, or particular conditions relating to extensions to cover beyond that in the normal policy.

6. **Other information,** including the basis of the premium and definition of the terms employed in the policy. This may often appear in the conditions section of the policy document.

9.4 ANALYSIS OF COVER

To meet the requirements of the risk management programme, the risk manager will require to analyse the terms and conditions of various covers to ensure they provide for the risks that have been identified and eliminate 'gaps' in cover.

9.4.1 Extent of Cover

The objective of an in-depth analysis of the policy cover is to discover:

- the circumstances under which the insurer will be responsible for the loss;

- the extent of the insurer's liability; and

- the requirements placed on the insured following a loss.

The policy should first be read quickly in its entirety in order to become familiar with its main provisions. Thereafter a closer examination can take place.

Williams and Heins in *Risk and Insurance* have suggested that the cover be examined under the headings of perils covered, property or source of liability covered, persons covered, losses covered, locations covered and time period covered. These headings form the outline of the check-list in Table 9.2 which is discussed on pages 198-200.

Table 9.2 – POLICY COVER CHECK-LIST

	YES	NO	Additional Information
Perils			
specified	|____|	|____|	List
all risks	|____|	|____|	
– exclusions	|____|	|____|	List
defined	|____|	|____|	State source
Property			
specified	|____|	|____|	List
blanket	|____|	|____|	
floating	|____|	|____|	
special extensions	|____|	|____|	List
Sources of Liability			
specified	|____|	|____|	List
comprehensive	|____|	|____|	
– exclusions	|____|	|____|	List
Persons			
other parties with insurable interest	|____|	|____|	List
can cover be extended?	|____|	|____|	
is cover assignable?	|____|	|____|	
Losses			
property			
– direct loss			
• damage	|____|	|____|	
• loss	|____|	|____|	
• other	|____|	|____|	Specify
– indirect loss			
• special extension	|____|	|____|	
– interruption loss	|____|	|____|	Specify how cover is arranged
– liability			
• comprehensive	|____|	|____|	Note exclusions
• specified	|____|	|____|	List
Time period			
annual renewal	|____|	|____|	Note date and time
more than 12 months	|____|	|____|	State renewal date
less than 12 months	|____|	|____|	State renewal date
Location			
specified	|____|	|____|	List
floating	|____|	|____|	
– exclusions	|____|	|____|	List
Special conditions under which cover would be terminated or suspended	|____|	|____|	Specify

9.4.1.1 Perils

Cover is arranged either on a specified or all risks basis. A specified policy lists only those risks against which cover is provided and may also contain a number of exclusions.

All risks cover applies to all perils except those listed as exclusions. Special care therefore has to be exercised to note those exclusions. Cover of course will not be available for perils which are excluded by the Courts, against public policy or intentionally incurred.

Careful note should be made of the definition of the perils covered as these may vary, especially in overseas markets.

9.4.1.2 Property

Cover is generally available for property by means of either a specified or a blanket policy. A blanket policy normally has three headings, for stock, plant, and buildings, in respect of each individual site or location. As the terms of the blanket policy require a regular declaration of the value of the property, this date should be noted as failure to comply may invalidate cover.

The terms of the cover should also be checked to determine whether certain expenses such as professional fees, additional expenditure incurred in compliance with local authority planning, building control and other regulations, and capital additions, etc. fall within the scope of cover. Normally they are not and would have to be arranged by means of an extension to the policy.

This also applies to the reinstatement of the sum insured condition subsequent to a loss, which would have to be added to the basic cover in a similar manner.

9.4.1.3 Sources of Liability

Cover can be arranged either in the form of a specified or combined/comprehensive cover. In either case the exclusions have to be examined carefully to determine where the burden of proof lies. For example a policy worded "claims arising from accidental injury or damage" places the onus upon the insured to prove that the accident was accidental. On the other hand, if the term "accidental" is omitted when referring to the injury, loss or damage covered, but "deliberate acts or omissions" are specifically excluded by means of a separate clause, the burden of proof shifts to the insurer to prove that the injury, damage, etc was not accidental.

9.4.1.4 Persons

This category refers to those persons in addition to the insured who have an interest in the policy. These can include joint or part owners of insured subjects, baillees or secured creditors. The insurer should be advised of such interests.

9.4.1.5 Losses

In most instances, with the notable exception of motor, the policy under examination will be concerned with providing cover for a particular class of exposure. However, policies written by different insurers for a particular class of exposure do not always provide identical cover, and note has to be made of any of these differences and of any extensions in respect of different losses or costs. For example:

Liability

The normal form of cover is for damages awarded against the insured in respect of injury to third parties or damage to their property, and legal costs incurred by the insured.

This cannot be presumed and should be checked, as there are some instances when cover does not extend to legal costs, or where only injury to the third party is covered. Furthermore, extensions are usually required:

- if retrospective cover for claims which occurred prior to the inception of the policy is desired;

- if cover in respect of other costs such as product recall and product guarantees is required. However, it should be noted that this cover is now extremely difficult to secure.

Business Interruption

Few companies can afford to ignore the consequences in terms of lost profits and 'temporary' increases in operating costs arising out of material damage. The manner in which this cover is provided should be noted as this may depend on the market in which the insurance is purchased. For example in the US interruption cover is usually incorporated in the form of an extension to existing property cover, whereas UK historical practice was to issue a separate policy – today this has changed. Differences in definitions between markets and policies, and the basis of cover should also be noted.

9.4.1.6 Location

Cover can be arranged either on the basis of a specific location or under the terms of a floating cover for all locations, other than those excluded. Points to note for specific locations are that all locations for which cover is required have been included. The points to note in respect of floating cover are (a) the excluded locations, and (b) that cover has been arranged for excluded locations.

9.4.1.7 Time Period

As the policy only indemnifies the insured for loss which arose, commenced or was caused during the period of cover, it is important that this period be carefully noted, particularly when the period of cover is other than the twelve month norm for non-life insurance. Dealing with overseas exposures requires that the differences in time zones be noted and that renewal dates and times be recorded accordingly.

9.4.2 Limits of Indemnity

The insurer seeks to limit liability of exposure to claims, the basis of which depends on whether the exposure is property or liability.

The insurer's liability for property is limited by the sum insured or limit of indemnity as specified by policy. This figure is the basis for the calculation of premium and the settlement of claims. It is important that this figure reflects current values since failure to do so will result in underinsurance, thereby reducing the value of the settlement when the condition of average is to be applied to the settlement figure.

Other points to check for include:

- Whether there is a reinstatement clause. A claim on the policy reduces the level of cover. This can be restored to its original level by means of the 'reinstatement' clause, which usually has to be specifically included at the inception of the policy at extra cost.

- Whether the requirements regarding updating of the sum insured under each heading of a blanket policy have been fulfilled, failure of which may invalidate cover.

- The arrangements to accommodate stock values within a blanket policy.

- Lower internal limits for specific items of cover in a blanket policy.

- Whether claims are settled in cash or in kind and the arrangements for doing so. Limitation of liability for liability exposures is usually a condition of the policy, the actual level being dependent upon (a) legislation, and (b) the experience of the insurer with regard to the nature and the stability of the costs in the particular area of cover. Historically in some instances, for example UK employer's liability (EL), insurers may have been prepared to offer unlimited cover. Today it is common practice to reflect the statutory limit of cover required.

The limit can be arranged on either a per event or annual aggregate basis. However, care should be taken in considering the potential to aggregate statutory class limits with other non-statutory classes of risk. For UK EL, for example, which now has a statutory limit requirement of £5m each occurrence, it is not possible to aggregate this exposure with other non-statutory classes of risk.

9.4.3 Responsibilities of the Insured

The policy conditions will normally place certain responsibilities on the insured in the event of a loss which have to be fulfilled in order to preserve its rights against the insurer. These should be noted and particular attention given to any unusual conditions. Whether the loss is property or liability, the insured is obliged to advise the insurer immediately of the occurrence of the loss followed by a more detailed account within seven to fourteen days, and is also expected to act in such a way as to reduce the loss. In the case of property damage this would include taking action to protect the property from further damage. Expenses incurred in this regard are usually reimbursed under the policy.

Liability claims whether as the result of an accident or arising from a claim, lawsuit or summons have to be advised to the insurer as above. The insured should advise the insurer when an accident which would be expected to give rise to claim occurs. The insured acts to reduce the loss by refusing to admit liability and gathering the information necessary to defend the claim.

The insured is usually expected to prove:

- that the loss is covered under the terms of the policy; and

- the amount of the loss.

For property damage, if the insured can provide proof of value, settlement will take place at that figure. In the absence of this the insurer will employ one of its own surveyors or appoint a loss adjuster. If the claim is large the insured can seek the services of a loss assessor to represent its position.

The value of liability exposures are set by the Courts. A loss however may not have occurred at the time of notification of the claim to the insurer as the award of damages may not yet have been made. The fact-gathering exercise is therefore a defensive move often undertaken with the insurer to seek to mitigate the size of the claim.

9.5 EVALUATION OF COVER

In section 9.2.2 we argued that insurance could be viewed as a series of cash flows arising at varying intervals between the insurer and the insured. The general pattern is an outflow at the beginning of the period of cover as the premium is paid, followed by a series of inflows as claims are settled. The time delay between the cash outflow and the final inflow can be considerable, as the timing of these inflows may in some cases extend well beyond the original period of cover.

9.5.1 Discounted Cash Flows in Insurance

The effect of the delay between the payment of the premium and the receipt of claim settlements can be incorporated in an evaluation of insurance cover by discounting the sums received from the insurer over the appropriate period of time.

Delays in settlement vary from one class of exposure to another. For example motor fleet accident and damage claims will be settled within a far shorter period than third party motor liability claims. Table 9.3 compiled by A M Best, the US insurance industry statistical organisation, shows the claims payout profile for US automobile liability.

Table 9.3 – AUTOMOBILE LIABILITY INSURANCE
Claim Payout Profile

Year	Paid (as % of claims notified)	Cumulative (%)
1	37.8	37.8
2	28.2	66.0
3	13.5	79.5
4	8.3	87.8
5	5.0	92.8
6	3.0	95.8
7	1.6	97.4
8	2.6	100.0

The table shows that all claims relating to a particular year took at least eight years to settle (year 8's figures include some claims settled in subsequent years). Less than 40% of claims were settled in the first year. Similar patterns exist for other forms of liability, although in some cases these may be even more pronounced. For example, in the above case it took three years to settle 80% of claims, it took five years to settle a similar proportion of US workers compensation liability claims.

Whilst these figures are drawn from US experience, the pattern of delay in settlement extending to more than eight years is by no means untypical for liability claims. European experience will be slightly different in terms of the actual periods involved, but the pattern will be similar.

Over a period of time these can assume a 'typical' pattern, varying according to the nature of the exposure, thus leading to the distinction between 'long tail' and 'short tail' business. We are going to illustrate this feature in the example below.

Note that the premium charged by the insurer is intended to recover claims and other running costs. In addition it will also include a contribution towards the insurer's profit and contingency reserves. The extent of these 'loadings' in respect of profit, expenses and reserves can vary from 10% – 60% according to the class of business.

For example: an employer's liability cover, premium for incoming year £75,000 (Tables 9.4 and 9.5).

Table 9.4 – CLAIMS SETTLEMENT PATTERN

Year 1	26%	Year 5	6%
Year 2	25%	Year 6	4%
Year 3	13%	Year 7	3%
Year 4	8%	Year 8	15%

Note: year 8 figures include losses settled in the eighth or subsequent years.

For the purposes of the example we shall assume that the premium figure is equal to the expected losses and that the actual experience will not vary widely from that figure. In addition, the rate of discount that has been chosen is 10% p.a., which reflects the opportunity cost of the cash spent on the premium. The rate could have been fixed in relation to the rate of return that the insurer was presumed to be earning on its investments.

Table 9.5 – CASH FLOW ANALYSIS

	Settlements	Discount Factor @ 10%	Present Value
	£		£
Premium	(75,000)	1.000	(75,000)
Year 1	19,500	0.9091	17,727
Year 2	18,750	0.8264	15,495
Year 3	9,750	0.7513	7,325
Year 4	6,000	0.6830	4,098
Year 5	4,500	0.6209	2,794
Year 6	3,000	0.5645	1,693
Year 7	2,250	0.5132	1,155
Year 8	11,250	0.4665	5,248
			(19,465)

The present value of the cost of claims to the insurer is £55,535 whereas it has received £75,000 in premium. From the buyer's point of view this represents a loss in present value terms of £19,465 on the financing of this exposure – a negative net present value. These calculations ignore the loadings for expenses, reserves and profit levied by the insurer.

The answer in this particular example depended on a number of factors including the method of premium payment, the claims settlement pattern and the rate of discount[1]. The assumption in this example that premium was paid at the beginning of the period of cover need not always be the case, as there are a number of different methods of paying premium.

9.5.2 Premium Payment Methods

Arrangements for payment of premium fall into the following categories:

(i) payable at inception;

(ii) payable at inception but subject to adjustment in the light of the underlying exposure;

(iii) payable in instalments;

(iv) payable retrospectively.

9.5.2.1 Payable at Inception

A single payment payable at the beginning of the policy period. Many covers are organised on this basis.

9.5.2.2 Adjustable

The initial premium payable at inception of the policy is based on an estimate of the exposure over the period concerned. At the end of the period an adjustment premium is paid to accommodate any change from the original estimate.

For example if employer's liability cover is rated according to the wage roll, this can only be estimated at the commencement of cover. By the end of the period, total wage costs will be known and the appropriate adjustment can be applied. Similar schemes can be used in fire insurance of stock, contractors' works damage, and money insurances.

The cash flow implication is that there will be at least two separate negative cash flows arising over a period of more than twelve months.

---

1 It should be noted that the selection of an appropriate discount rate will vary from time to time depending on the prevailing interest rate environment. This example is simply to demonstrate the effect of discounting of cashflows.

9.5.2.3 *Payable in Instalments*

The large negative outflow of the premium payable at inception is now replaced by a series of smaller outflows over the period of cover, the number and the timing of which affects the value of the cover purchased. If the insurer makes an additional charge for this facility it should be included in the calculations.

9.5.2.4 *Retrospective Plans*

In contrast to the previous cases, retrospective premiums are based on loss experience rather than underlying exposure. This method of premium may be more attractive to a risk management conscious company with a good loss record.

The premium will vary between certain specified limits according to loss experience. This provides a measure of protection against poorer than expected loss experience.

A deposit premium is paid at the outset with further adjustments based on loss experience being made at agreed intervals. These adjustments occur either on the expiry of the period of insurance or in relation to the settlement of claims. In the latter case the adjustment period for some exposures like liability may range from four to seven years.

The cash flow position is more complex under a retrospective arrangement due to the larger number and varied timings of the negative flows. The principle of analysis remains the same, however: only cash flows are relevant; and these can be discounted to their present value whether they are negative or positive.

Retros are not suitable for widespread use. The general criteria are:

- there must be a large number of small to medium claims per annum; and
- there is a large spread of independent exposure units.

The classes of insurance most suited to retro policies include employer's liability, cargo, aviation, motor, and group life. It is not suitable for products or public liability, or fire cover except in carefully defined circumstances.

The current insurer appetite towards retrospectively rated arrangements is low. Fixed premium offerings are much more attractive to the insurance market with a desire to maximise up-front cashflows and current premium volumes.

9.5.3 Discounting Quarterly and Monthly Cash Flows

The claims settlement pattern in the example assumed annual cash flows. It is unlikely that this will always be the case, either for claims or even premium in some instances. As cash flows can be discounted for periods of less than a year it is also possible to analyse cover for 'short tail' business. (See Chapter 2 Section 2.5.3 for discounting periods of less than 1 year.) Consider the following example which concerns motor accidental damage cover (Table 9.6).

Expected monthly motor accident damage claims for the coming year are £9,860. Claims are settled three months in arrears. The premium of £118,320 is payable at inception.

Table 9.6 – CASH FLOW ANALYSIS

	Claim Incurred £	Settled £	Discount Factor @ 12% p.a.	Present Value £
Premium		–	1.0000	(118,320)
Jan	9,860	–		–
Feb	9,860	–		–
Mar	9,860	–		–
Apr	9,860	9,860	0.9610	9,475
May	9,860	9,860	0.9515	9,382
Jun	9,860	9,860	0.9420	9,288
Jul	9,860	9,860	0.9327	9,196
Aug	9,860	9,860	0.9235	9,106
Sept	9,860	9,860	0.9143	9,015
Oct	9,860	9,860	0.9053	8,926
Nov	9,860	9,860	0.8963	8,838
Dec	9,860	9,860	0.8874	8,750
Jan		9,860	0.8787	8,664
Feb		9,860	0.8700	8,578
Mar		9,860	0.8613	8,492
				(10,610)

The constant monthly loss figure has been assumed for the purposes of illustration, as has the fact that the level of pure losses is equal to the premium charged. (Note that the discount factor begins in month 4 because claims are settled three months in arrears.) However, even where there are no profit or expense loadings, the insurer continues to 'profit' from the risk in present value terms. Although this assumes that the loss experience will not be worse than expected, neither does it allow for better than expected loss experience.

All insurance contracts can be analysed in this manner to reveal the financial worth of insurance to the purchaser. The result as we have seen depends on the premium arrangement, the claims settlement pattern and rate of discount selected. The premium arrangements are a matter for negotiation between the insured and the insurer and the pattern of settlements is a matter for observation from past experience. Choice of the rate of discount requires consultation with financial management.

Discounted cash flow analysis therefore enables one cover to be compared with another on the same basis. Furthermore, it makes it possible to compare insurance with other methods of funding. However, the previous comments regarding the selection of an appropriate 'current' discount rate refers – see Footnote 1 page 205 relating to Table 9.5.

10

INSURANCE (2)
INSURANCE NEEDS
AND PROGRAMMES

10.1 INTRODUCTION

In the previous chapter we concentrated on examination of the terms and value of cover; in this chapter we extend the analysis to the insurance programme as a whole. This will involve determining the insurance needs and reviewing current programmes; considering approaches to dealing with the exposures of the multinational corporation; and the appraisal and selection of brokers.

10.2 DETERMINATION OF INSURANCE NEEDS

Before any judgment of whether current insurance arrangements meet the organisational requirements, it is necessary firstly to determine the organisation's insurable exposures. The nature of these exposures is governed by the organisation's productive activities, its contractual commitments, and the legal requirements it has to meet as part of its statutory obligations.

If a review of risk management exposures has been carried out, this will provide the basic information for the review of insurances. In the absence of this, the following facts relating to the organisation should be ascertained:

- nature of activities;
- location;
- assets;
- employees;

- customers;

- suppliers.

Table 10.1 is a checklist of these needs together with their insurance implications and requirements. It is based on the analysis of insurance needs in the *Handbook of Risk Management*.

An analysis of this nature would reveal the organisation's major areas of exposure and the balance between them. For example the exposures of a manufacturing organisation, where a substantial proportion of economic activity is carried out on the premises, will be different from those of an organisation whose employees are employed largely on the premises of others.

Table 10.1 – ANALYSING INSURANCE NEEDS

Checklist	Insurance Implications
Economic Activity • nature of the operations of the organisation and subsidiaries where appropriate • location of the centres of economic activity, i.e. whether these are 'on-site' or 'off-site'	All activities have to be identified. They determine the type and extent of insurances required. This can affect the type and extent of liability insurances required, as well as extensions to fire and property policies to cover tools, etc used away from premises.
Assets (physical and financial, including records) • geographical location and situation • values at risk (based on replacement or reinstatement values) • are they owned, leased, or held on behalf of a third party? • perils to which property is exposed	Of relevance to geographical coverage, limits of indemnity of property and liability insurances. Leasing, hire agreements and service contracts have to be checked to determine responsibilities and insurance requirements.
Customers • identity • range • percentage value of business per customer including dependence on a particular customer • location • terms and conditions of contracts – i.e. credit terms and transfer of liabilities • nature of relationship with customer	Determines extent of product liability and professional indemnity insurances required. Care to be exercised to ensure that contract terms do not breach insurer's conditions. Credit insurance is available for domestic and export sales. Export credit insurance can also be arranged to cover political risk.
Suppliers • identity • location • percentage value of business • contract terms as above • alternative sources	As above for customers.

Business Interruption
 	
• events leading to interruption of operations
 	
• factors affecting the severity of the disruption
  – the extent of organisational interdependence
  – dependence on suppliers of power, water and other services, materials, etc
  – dependence on particular customers
	Perils covered, extension of cover to suppliers and duration of cover.

Employees • general organisational policy with respect to employee benefits • key personnel in terms of organisational performance or whose fraudulent actions could lead to substantial loss	Cover can be arranged for permanent health, travel and medical expenses insurance. Life and accident insurances could be arranged to compensate the company for loss of services. Fidelity guarantee insurance may be required to cover this area.

10.2.1 Compulsory Insurances

There are certain circumstances where the purchase of insurance is mandatory. This may arise as the result of contractual commitments or legislation.

10.2.1.1 Contractual Commitments

The contractual commitments can be due either to third parties or the insurer. One form of contractual commitment to the insurer may arise out of a long term agreement upon which a premium discount is based. Another is where an organisation is required to arrange insurance as the result of a contract condition. For instance, where mortgage and debenture deeds require that the assets over which they are secured are adequately insured; or in the standard form of building contract which stipulates the purchase of insurance cover.

The risk manager will have to ensure that any contractual conditions stipulating the purchase of insurance are advised to him, that the conditions are complied with, and that the insurer is advised of any additional liabilities that are assumed as a result.

10.2.1.2 Legislation

Legislation affecting insurance may concern either insurances which have to be purchased or insurers with whom business can be placed. Regulations concerning these vary from country to country. Organisations with operations spanning national boundaries have to acquaint themselves with these regulations and any changes that take place from time to time. Many organisations in this position will tend to rely on the advice of an insurance broker with experience of insurance markets in the areas concerned. The problem of arranging insurances for the multinational corporation will be taken further in section 10.5 below.

10.3 REVIEW OF INSURANCE PROGRAMME

Periodically the risk manager will have to carry out a review of the corporate risk financing programme, either as a result of organisational requirements or as a matter of risk management policy. This process has to be distinguished from the renewal process where, in the absence of good reasons to the contrary, short term renewable covers are placed with the same carrier as in the previous period. The purpose of the review is a thorough appraisal of the current arrangements in the light of both current and potential exposures, to verify the value of the insurance programme and consider other courses of action, such as increasing levels of retention or using alternative risk financing tools.

A review of this nature should only be carried out every three to five years. Any more frequent and it may prove counter-productive in terms of relationships with insurers and the market. Moreover, it represents a major commitment of resources, as the timeframe from initiation to placement of the risks in the market can vary from three to six months. Nevertheless, in the current hard market environment a more frequent review may be necessary.

Use of a broker or a risk management consultant is generally recommended at the review stage, to provide technical services which may not be available in-house, and outside expert opinion. It is beneficial to have the views of more than one intermediary but because of the time required to brief them and consider their reports, the numbers involved should be limited to three or four. Moreover, the size of the programme and the nature of the major exposures may require the services of one or more brokers for placement of the full risk programme. One of these will probably require to be a Lloyd's broker.

In dealings with consultants or brokers, the role of the risk manager would typically include:

- establishment of the criteria for selection of intermediaries, insurers and ancillary services;

- analysis of the loss exposures – probably in co-operation with the intermediary – and identification of suitable covers in the market;

- participation where required in the presentation of the risk to the market;

- to assist in negotiation of the terms of the insurance contract and premium rates; and

- co-ordinating functions within the group which will have input to the risk finance process.

10.3.1 Review of Current Insurances

Part of the review will include a reappraisal of the insurances currently in place. A report of insurance premiums and claims experience for the previous three to five years would have to be prepared covering the following areas:

- premium expenditure analysed according to:
  - line of cover;
  - country, region or location;
  - subsidiary, division or operating group;
  - insurer or insurers underwriting the risk noting the lines covered;
  - brokers, noting line of cover and commission or fee received.

- each class of exposure analysed according to:
  - location;
  - subsidiary, division and company;
  - sum insured and EMLs or limit of indemnity, noting the existence of deductibles and other risk sharing agreements;
  - major exposures;
  - perils covered.

- claims according to:
  - location;
  - subsidiary, division and company;
  - line of cover;
  - size (claims or loss ratio);
  - causation.

The outcome of this review can be compared with the results from the analysis of the insurance needs as outlined in table 10.1 to discern gaps or overlaps in cover. The organisation's brokers may also be able to assist in this process.

10.3.2 Presentation of the Risk to the Market

Once the review of the programmes is complete, the organisation will want to seek a price for cover it has identified is required from the market. To do this it will have to prepare a specification of its exposures for submission to the market.

In general the specification should move from the general to the specific as noted below:

- a detailed summary of information relevant to the risk; today underwriters require much more information than in previous years. The requirement for detail should not be underestimated.

- details of the aggregate losses incurred for each major line of insurance for a minimum of three to five years of experience.

- details of individual significant losses.

- analysis of particular losses.

- note made of any unusual circumstances affecting either:

  - the loss experience; or
  - the exposures for the incoming period of cover together with requests for especially high limits of coverage.

- describe the existing insurance programme and premiums.

- list additional sources of technical information.

- a covering letter detailing the time schedule for negotiation and implementation of the programme.

The contents of the specification should be presented in logical order. An example of the contents of a liability insurance specification is given in Table 10.2. It should be noted that increasingly the risk manager's ability to present/supply this information in an electronic format is important to underwriters, captive managers and brokers/consultants.

Table 10.2 – TABLE OF CONTENTS FOR UNDERWRITING SPECIFICATIONS

A   Description of Operations

1. Overview of operations by subsidiaries, divisions and branches
2. Financial Statement
3. Annual Report

B   Description of Risk Management Department

1. Philosophy
2. Organisation and structure
3. Functions/services provided – e.g. costs allocation, claims handling, loss prevention, etc
4. Services contracted to external vendors

C   Property Exposure Analysis

1. Basis and date of valuation
2. Total values by location and line of coverage
3. Estimated maximum loss (EML and any other measures PML, MPL, etc) and the sum insured by location
4. Individual fire protection COPE data, pictures and diagrams for large locations
5. Values for property in transit and in scheduled locations
6. Business interruption worksheets with basis of calculations
7. Other time element value estimates
8. Full post or zip code listings
9. Survey reports

D   Liability Exposure Analysis

1. Quantified underwriting data: revenues, payrolls, advertising expenditure, etc
2. Detailed description of products which develop exposures
3. All other exposures
   (a) care custody and control situations
   (b) professional liability
   (c) potential liabilities under statutory provisions
   (d) ships and aircraft
   (e) other perceived exposures
   (f) terrorism exposure information
   (g) contractual liability exposure

E   Loss Analysis

1. Description of claims handling: insurer, in-house or contracted out
2. Total incurred losses by line of coverage
3. Description of large claims (specified in advance) including those not settled
4. Severity distribution of losses by line of cover and in total
5. Loss forecasting and retention analysis
6. Causation analysis

F   Detailed Cover Specification

1. Property exposures
2. Business interruption exposures
3. Liability exposures

G   Timetable Requirements

10.3.3 Selection of Insurers

It is unlikely that, when there are a number of competing suppliers in the market, the cover offered by each will be identical. An appraisal of the various covers by means of a clause by clause comparison can be made in the manner suggested by Bannister and Bawcutt and illustrated in Table 10.3. Alternatively the comparison could be based on the checklist presented in Table 9.2 in Chapter 9.

Table 10.3 – PRODUCTION LIABILITY INSURANCES COMPARISON

Conditions of Cover	COMPANY		
	A	B	C
1.			
2.			
3.			
4.			

10.4 INSURANCE INTERMEDIARIES

One of the distinctive features of the insurance market is the presence of the intermediary – the insurance broker. With the notable exception of Lloyd's, the use of an insurance broker to place risks with the market is not mandatory. Many firms typically deal direct with a few insurers for certain covers and will employ one or two brokers to handle the remainder of the insurers. Since it is possible in most instances to deal direct with the market, the use of a broker has to be justified in terms of the value added by the broker to what would have been received direct from the insurer.

Bannister and Bawcutt in *Practical Risk Management* (Witherby) suggest the use of the broker should lead to an overall improvement in financial performance due to the reduction in insurance costs achieved through:

- a review of risk handling arrangements to ensure the proper handling of risk exposures through a combination of insurance and non-insurance measures;

- reduction in the level of insured and non-insured losses;

- more effective insurance purchasing than could be arranged direct with insurers.

In addition to this brokers add value through:

- benefits of peer experience;

- market knowledge and leverage;

- programme design expertise.

To fulfil these requirements the range of services which a broker would have to provide would include:

- a review of pure risk exposures;

- an evaluation of the current risk financing programme in the light of the results of the review of pure risk exposures, together with recommendations for the handling of these exposures.

This is of particular importance if available policy wordings do not match the exposures under consideration. From experience, the broker may be able to have policy wordings tailored to suit the needs of the client. This is especially valuable when the client has world-wide operations where knowledge of local market conditions is necessary to meet the needs of the insured.

The proposed risk financing plan should also incorporate the level of losses that could be financed from its own resources:

- the provision of advice on loss prevention and reduction measures across the range of exposures, and where necessary assistance in their implementation;

- the purchase of insurance on behalf of the client having regard to the premium, cover, services (surveys, etc), documentation and claims procedures, and the solvency and stability of the insurer; and

- claims handling and negotiation of settlements and recoveries.

10.4.1 Selection of Brokers

The choice of a broker is important because of the potential added value that selection of a firm with services and expertise appropriate to the needs of the organisation can bring. The organisation requires to establish a system to assist in selection of a suitable broker or brokers.

The basic criterion of such a selection is the extent to which various candidates match the profile of the buyer. The system requires an analysis of:

- the organisation and its needs;

- the broker's structure, organisation and strengths.

The analysis of the firm's needs can be based on the results of earlier investigations if they have been carried out, covering such areas as:

- the size of the organisation, expressed for example in terms of turnover, number of employees, asset values, etc;

- the geographical location of major operations and their geographical spread;

- the principal activities of the organisation;

- potential areas of exposure;

- analysis of losses by line of cover and location;

- identification of the main weaknesses in loss control;

- structure and performance of the risk management and insurance department;

- analysis of insurance costs:
  - premium expenditure by line of cover and location;
  - major losses; and
  - evaluation of claims experience in relation to premium costs.

The analysis of brokers should concentrate on:

- size, spread and location of offices;
- specialist experience and strengths;
- the quality and experience of staff handling and placing the business in the market;
- services to be provided, their frequency and additional or special services offered.

The purpose of the analyses is to determine the suitability of the respective broker to the needs of the organisation and whether the strengths and services coincide with the organisation's weaknesses and needs. The various brokers can then be ranked on a pre-determined scale according to the following criteria and the selection made.

(i) Is the size of the broker, its technical services and the spread of its operations relevant to the risk profile of the company?

(ii) Is there staff in sufficient numbers and of sufficient quality to carry out what is required of them?

(iii) Do the guaranteed services meet the needs of the organisation?

(iv) How does the provision of additional services compare with those of competitors?

(v) How does the broker's strengths and expertise match the perceived needs and problems of the organisation?

(vi) What is the cost in relation to the services provided and in comparison to competitors?

Increasingly risk managers may need to look for industry specialisation within broking houses as well as innovation in the area of programme design.

The method is subjective but it forces the risk manager to evaluate the services offered and the return received in exchange for fees paid.

10.4.2 Remuneration of Intermediaries

Brokers have traditionally operated on a commission basis but latterly moves have been made towards payment on a fee basis. This has been prompted by a number of pressures including:

- buyers critical of the conflict of interests faced by a broker dependent on commission when advising on a risk financing programme;

- the fact that the effort required to place a risk is not directly related to premium volume and that brokers provided many services not related to premium volume;

- brokers are better protected against swings in the underwriting cycle than insurers, because the inverse relationship between the volume of business and premium level reduces the variability in broker earnings: if premiums rise less cover is purchased but at higher rates and vice versa;

- as commission is paid by insurers the true cost of risk and the costs of handling risk are obscured.

Moving to a negotiated fee system means that the buyer has to come to an agreement with the intermediary and pay directly for the service provided. This identifies the exact level of these costs, compensates the broker for the effort expended and allows greater objectivity in recommendations regarding risk financing techniques. However it involves the buyer in work and expense which had previously been subsumed under the heading of insurance costs.

A number of variations on these basic themes have been introduced. These include:

- sliding scale of commissions based on premium income paid by insurers to brokers. This recognises the earlier point concerning the volume of work required by the broker in relation to the premium volume;

- commission plus fee. Commission for the arrangement of insurances is levied at a lower rate than normal with consultancy and other services being charged on a fee basis. Fees can be negotiated on a project or annual basis or both;

- a compensation system under which

  - the buyer agrees to pay an annual fee at the end of the financial period, the amount being the minimum required by the broker to provide the services envisaged for the year;
  - the broker retains all commissions received from insurers during the year;

– at the year-end, if commissions received from insurers are less than the amount agreed, the insured has to pay the balance; if the sums received are greater the broker retains the excess.

10.5 INSURANCE OF MULTINATIONAL CORPORATIONS

The multinational corporation has a number of additional considerations regarding the arrangement of its insurances by virtue of its operations in a number of sovereign territories. These include:

- differences in legislation with respect to insurance arrangements;

- operating relationships between the parent and subsidiaries; and

- in some cases a hostile political climate towards its presence leads to an alteration in its relationship with insurers and brokers.

The following differences in insurance operations have been observed to operate in various countries:

(i) Insurance and general legislation.

(ii) Taxation.

(iii) Insurance market conditions.

(iv) Covers.

(v) Ancillary services.

(vi) Reinsurance regulations.

(vii) Relationship between the host government and the insurance market.

There are other circumstances which are not confined to risk financing but which affect or restrict the organisation's freedom to organise and administer its insurance programmes, including exchange controls, language, culture, attitude of the host government to multinational corporations, and a self-imposed obligation by the organisation to purchase in local markets where these can provide the service or product required.

10.5.1 Insurance Legislation

Insurance legislation covers such areas as the ownership and control of insurance businesses, authorisation of insurers to operate in the local market and reinsurance business.

10.5.1.1 Ownership and Control of Insurers

In some countries only publicly owned or nationalised insurers are permitted to operate. In others the restrictions may require a minimum percentage of local ownership. In either event the existing relationship with the parent's insurers is not effective or constrained.

10.5.1.2 Insurance Regulations

These can include licensing requirements, control over insurers authorised to write business in the local market, and the nature of compulsory insurances.

Licensing regulations can stipulate solvency requirements that discriminate in favour of locally based insurers, thus restricting the multinational's freedom of choice.

The host government may also prohibit or strictly control the transaction of unauthorised or non-admitted business. Where a country prohibits non-admitted insurers this may render the receipt of payments in respect of non-admitted covers illegal. Furthermore, there is a risk that the contract will not be recognised in the courts of the country of the subsidiary.

Another area of government involvement is in the determination of which insurances are compulsory and whether these have to be placed in the local market.

Specifically for Europe has been the development of passporting ability for EU based insurers within Europe. Both UK and European law determine the UK regulatory structure. Much European law looks to create a single, competitive and efficient European market.

The Insurance Directives (INSD) are one of the key financial services directives. The central feature is the facilitation of cross border business and the opening of branch offices. This is done through a 'passport'.

Passporting is permitted within the European Economic Area (EU plus Norway, Iceland and Liechtenstein).

This provides the ability for an insurer operating out of one country to legitimately do business in another. The entity remains to be regulated by the home Country State but must also contact the Host State in order to do business.

10.5.1.3 Reinsurance

Even if the multinational corporation has to place covers in the local market it can still seek to participate in its own risks through reinsuring, by means of a captive, the risks ceded by the local market. This however may be frustrated if local regulations require that these be placed with the state reinsurer.

10.5.2 Local Insurance Market Arrangements

Areas of concern for the multinational corporation in relation to the operation of the local insurance markets are:

- whether the local market has a single insurer with sufficient capacity to support the needs of the subsidiary. This problem may require alternative arrangements such as co-insurance to meet the multinational corporation's needs;

- the adequacy of the local market's indemnity and liability limits in relation to the exposures of the subsidiary;

- whether a tariff agreement operates, for which lines of cover and the effect this has on the price of the cover;

- the practice and existence of long term agreements (ten years in some cases) or tacit renewal clauses which restricts the parent's freedom of action if it is seeking to implement a global risk financing programme.

10.5.3 Cover

There may also be variations in the conditions of cover. Some exposures may not be covered in the general conditions accepted by the market. There may also be differences in the definitions of certain exposures. The main problem exists where the coverage in the local market is narrower than is available from the non-admitted insurer, although there are exceptions to this rule.

10.5.4 Services

The provision and quality of ancillary services such as loss adjustment, risk surveys, and loss prevention services will also vary from market to market. In some cases they may be provided by the insurer, in others by independent agencies. The quality of provision and the standards of physical risk control expected will also vary.

10.5.5 Taxation

There may be discriminatory tax provisions against non-admitted insurance such as non-deductibility of premiums against tax liabilities. The effect of this is to effectively increase the cost of insurance as premiums are paid out of after-tax income. Premiums may also be subject to premium taxes, further increasing the effective cost. Finally, remittances from non-admitted insurers in respect of claims settlements – where these are permissible – may also be subject to import taxes in addition to the normal taxation of income.

10.5.6 Multinational Insurances

In addition to the problems of the differences of the insurance market, the multinational corporation is also faced with a number of others in the organisation, administration and control of its risk financing programme. These include conflicts which arise between the requirements of the parent and the subsidiary, ensuring consistency of cover, and maintaining control over the insurance programme given the wide range of operations.

The conflict between the parent and the subsidiary will in part be a function of the structure of the organisation and its management style. It may be likely that the requirements of the parent for some form of centralised control over such matters as premium costs and local deductible levels conflict with the requirements for a degree of local autonomy in these areas.

The difficulties associated with maintaining control over cover and ensuring its consistency are related to the problems of the relationship between central and local management and the scale of the operations of a multinational corporation. In practical terms, a moderate sized multinational corporation may have operations in ten separate countries, with an average of five subsidiaries in each country. This means fifty separate companies' programmes which have to be co-ordinated. If we assume five to ten separate lines of cover for each company, this can amount to between two hundred and fifty to five hundred separate policies, each with their own terms and conditions – in at least ten different languages!

These practical difficulties and those associated with the arrangement of insurances have led to the recognition of the need for co-ordinated multinational insurance programmes to meet the needs of the multinational corporation. Notwithstanding the problems of infringing local autonomy, centralisation of the global insurance programme does bestow a number of benefits such as consistency and economy.

10.5.6.1 Benefits of a Co-ordinated Programme

The co-ordinated programme should permit consistency in terms of the conditions of cover and limits, and should eliminate or at least reduce overlaps and gaps in cover. There will also be consistent approach to the levels of self-insurance to be borne, in addition to which the role of the captive can be more clearly defined. Finally, consistency of provision and quality of technical services such as loss analysis, claims handling, and the placement of insurances can also be maintained.

The purchasing power of the multinational corporation can be utilised in the co-ordinated programme, rather than dissipating it through a large number of smaller transactions through the equivalent of the 'bulk-buying' discount. Underwriters have and may be willing to accept the global risk provided it is well spread and there is a good loss record. Evidence of good risk management practice and capabilities will also strengthen the multinational corporation's case. The corporation itself can also benefit from combining its risk through a group deductible. As the group will be able to sustain a larger deductible than an individual operating unit, this feature should be exploited to increase premium savings and release cash. A centralised programme also makes it possible to develop a system to allocate premium to operating units in accordance with their loss experience, thus providing another tool for the control of risk.

10.5.6.2 Co-ordinated Multinational Insurance Programmes

The main forms of co-ordinated programme are:

(i) a programme of local insurance covers in the various locations issued by the same insurer: this is known as a fully admitted programme;

(ii) a non-admitted programme in which insurance cover for all corporate assets regardless is purchased by the parent, on parent country defined terms and conditions;

(iii) a combined programme in which admitted cover is purchased through local programmes, but differences in cover and limits of indemnity are supplemented with a central Difference in Cover (DIC)/Difference in Limits (DIL) policy purchased in the country of the parent.

Fully admitted programme

The benefits of a fully admitted programme are that a full scope programme is available from the insurer in the local market and that the exposures are rated on a uniform basis. The local company is in turn able to benefit from the tax deductibility of the premiums and there is no currency risk to the group. The principal drawback to the insured is the differences in policy wordings that exist in the various localities, thus requiring more careful scrutiny and control. The insurer is also faced with high administrative costs of maintaining establishments in the potentially wide range of locations of clients.

Full non-admitted programme

Both the insurer and the insured reap the benefits of large scale under such a programme. A comprehensive programme of cover for all locations can be arranged centrally on the terms and conditions in the country of the parent, thus leading to reduction in administration and control and also economy of handling costs. The greater purchasing power of the buyer in the market enables it to bargain a competitive price from the supplier. The wider spread of risk and larger number of exposure units also enables the use of experience rated programmes.

These benefits of economy and simplicity of administration have to be balanced against the problems of such programmes, as their use is prohibited in a large number of territories. In addition to questions over their legality they will not be deductible against local taxes, the parent may not be able to charge the premium back to the subsidiary, the parent may not in some instances be able to charge the portion of the premium relating to 'foreign' risks against profits, and the subsidiary may have to bear additional tax liabilities on the funds remitted in respect of the loss.

Moreover, there will also be currency risks due to the delay between occurrence of the claim and its settlement, in addition to the costs of remitting funds to the subsidiary. Finally, under the centralised arrangement the insurer does not provide a local service to the subsidiary and there may be inadequate cover of specific local exposures.

Combined programme

The obvious compromise is to structure a programme which takes advantage of the benefits of locally placed insurances, whilst providing the levels of protection normally enjoyed in the country of the parent, and avoiding the difficulties of the exclusive use of non-admitted insurances where these are prohibited. The main forms of co-ordinated programmes are:

- an integrated programme comprising a 'master' global policy with DIC and DIL provisions supported by 'primaries' issued at local level, all issued by the same insurer. The 'master' and 'primaries' are both issued by the same insurer;

- a co-ordinated programme which has the same structure as the integrated programme but which uses different insurers;

- a 'twin towers' programme designed specifically to handle North American exposures. In this case the North American exposures are separated out from the rest of the programme. The remainder of the programme is then arranged as a conventional integrated or co-ordinated programme. The programme can be placed with either a single or two insurers.

The DIC cover is used to supplement local wordings and to extend it where applicable, to include for example full extended coverage in respect of property damage arising from earthquake, strike, riot and civil commotion, or liability damages from products, product recall, or motor. The benefits are similar to those enjoyed under the full non-admitted programme, in addition to which the following also apply:

- reduced currency risk and remittance costs of claims payouts, as the majority of these are settled locally;

- local country perils are included in the programme; and

- a substantial part of the premium costs are tax deductible in the country of risk.

There are still a number of problems with this approach. The flexibility of the programme may be inhibited by the operation of the tariff in some countries and the use of experience based rating may increase premiums in some locations, making the programme less desirable locally. The currency risks and remittance costs remain for non-admitted losses in respect of differences in conditions perils. Finally, the premium costs may not be tax deductible and in some cases it may not be possible to recover the costs of the DIC cover from the subsidiary.

10.5.6.3 Requirements of Insurers and Brokers

Global insurance programmes for multinationals place many requirements on brokers and insurers. For the insurer, among the more important of these would be:

- representation in each of the countries in which the client operates;

- access to reinsurance facilities;

- organisational structure to co-ordinate administration of a world-wide programme;

- ability to vet the security of reinsurers;

- consistent world-wide engineering and technical services;

- consistent claims management service;

- consistent and uniform quality of cover;

- competitive and flexible response to requests for tailored central coverage, especially for catastrophe protection;

- local authorisation and flexibility of cover.

The broker should be represented in all the major areas in which the client is involved and demonstrate an understanding of the needs of the client and their relationship to the programme both globally and locally. It should be capable of co-ordinating the world-wide programme and reporting directly to the risk manager, and be able to provide advisory, consultancy and technical services at both central and local level.

The broker will be expected to provide a wide range of services including:

- captive management;

- loss control services and consultancy;

- technical and market briefings;

- risk management consultancy;

- broking of risk, including negotiation of DIC, catastrophe, and locally admitted cover;

- local representation.

10.6 SUMMARY AND CONCLUSION

Insurance still remains the most widely used risk financing tool. It is important therefore to ensure that the structure of the programme and the terms of the cover meet the needs and exposures of the organisation. A soundly managed programme has to demonstrate that it provides protection for balance sheet values at economic cost. Review of the entire programme covering exposures, premiums and claims experience for a three to five year period should therefore be carried out on a regular basis.

The problems of a multinational corporation are particularly complex. Currency movements, language, culture, insurance legislation, and policy wordings combine to complicate the arrangement, implementation and control of insurance programmes which cover a number of sovereign territories. This has led to the development of co-ordinated programmes to integrate insurance arrangements at subsidiary and head office level within an overall framework.

Most organisations look to the insurance broker for support in at least some of its dealings with the market. This is almost mandatory in the case of multinational insurance programmes. Where a broker is appointed, the arrangement should be cost effective and subject to minimum servicing and quality requirements. The buyer may wish to consider pursuing remuneration of the broker on a fee rather than commission basis.

11

ALTERNATIVE RISK FINANCE

11.1 INTRODUCTION

The interest in Alternative Risk Finance (ARF) has grown dramatically since the start of the 1990s. ARF now implies something more than the use of captives or of large self-insured retentions. Indeed, it could be argued that some of these techniques are now so commonplace that they have become mainstream and thus, by definition, cannot be 'alternative'.

11.2 PRIMARY ARF STRUCTURES

So far the trend has been for a more focused range of products and services, which are all designed to address significant risks which a company wishes to either retain or transfer. These are not just the traditional uninsurable fortuitous hazard risks, but include issues ranging from revenue stabilisation to the capping of legacy liabilities for uninsurable risks in merger and acquisition activities.

Before discussing some of the particular structures it is important to consider some of the limitations of pure risk retention and pure risk transfer.

Limitations on risk retention:

- contractual partners such as banks require that insurance is purchased to protect their interests;
- management concerns over the perception of investors should there be a need to make recourse to additional equity or debt if unexpected losses occur;
- the lack of short term cash flow to meet major loss payments;
- the inability to spread the economic (cash) impact of a loss over

time due to budgeting constraint.

Limitations on risk transfer:

- lack of available markets willing to accept the contractual liability for risk or imposing exclusions;

- limitations on the financial capacity of third parties who will accept the risk;

- concerns over the financial strength of third parties that are willing to accept the risk;

- limitations on the time period over which a third party will accept transfer. For example, a company taking on a five-year contract may only be able to transfer the risk on an annual basis.

These limitations can be summarised into five key areas that need to be addressed:

1. Third parties require that the company evidences a contract of risk transfer, but the organisation views the cost of the contract as too high and would rather retain the risk.

2. Management is concerned about the impact on investors' perception of a loss that is retained when it could have been transferred to a third party, even though it perceives the transfer not to be cost effective.

3. A company would like to maintain its annual cash flow performance against the impact of an unexpected loss.

4. A company would like to insulate its short-term cash flow needs against the impact of an unexpected loss.

5. A company is concerned that a third party may not be financially strong enough to meet the potential loss should it occur.

In attempting to address these five key issues, the proponents of ARF solutions have developed a number of possible approaches. It must be stressed that some of these particular products are no longer utilised due to changing needs and regulations, but studying past and present products puts the future into perspective:

- time and distance policies;

- spread loss policies;

- alternative or financial reinsurance, or finite risk;

- hybrids; and

- chronological stabilisation programmes.

There are no hard and fast definitions of any of these products and the student may come across more than one of the above definitions in everyday business affairs. It is their characteristics that classify them – particularly, the recognition that money has a time value. However, the term 'finite risk' is generally considered the most common term for these types of structure and will encompass most of the following features, in an attempt to meet the five key limitations in the order they were discussed above:

- the contracts are generally structured as insurance contracts which, whilst limiting the exposure of the insurer (hence the term 'finite'), do actually provide risk transfer and thus are classified as insurance contracts;

- as an insurance contract, the company receives income from a third party to meet claims that should meet the immediate concerns of investors and therefore management;

- finite structures tend to have a multi-year contract term. The insured pays premiums over a number of financial years (normally between 3 and 5) to secure a coverage limit, which is in most cases fully available for a single or multiple losses in a single year. This structure can in many circumstances allow a company to spread the economic (cash) impact of a loss or losses across a number of years;

- the longer-term contract may include some acceleration of payments in the event of a loss, however it is usual that an insured will be able to achieve significant smoothing of cash flow payments;

- the providers of these structures are generally A+ or above rated insurers and are therefore the most secure markets available.

11.2.1 Structuring of a Finite Risk Arrangement

Fig. 11.1

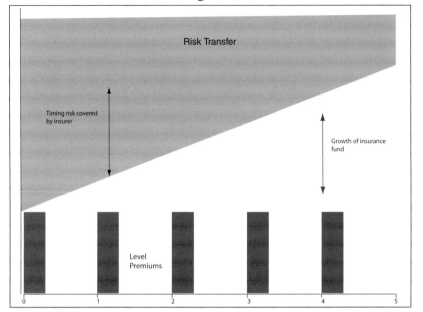

If appropriate, a suitable deductible would be put in place, which either a captive or the insured themselves should retain. The division of retention between the insured and the captive can be tailored to fit in with the business aims and internal sensitivities of the organisation at the time.

As illustrated in Figure 11.1, a finite layer with an element of risk transfer would be structured in excess of the deductible. Funding for the finite layer would be on an annual basis, with a premium instalment payable at inception and each subsequent year of the programme.

Typically the pre-loss funding would use the basis of an 'Experience Account' with a partner insurer, whereby upon payment of the premium a defined percentage, say 70%, would be credited to the insured's 'Experience Account'. The remaining 30% represents the insurer's margin and risk premium.

Investment income would accumulate on the Experience Account. For example this could be at a rate of LIBOR[1] minus 100 basis points.

1   LIBOR – London Interbank Offered Rate

All losses would be paid from the insured's Experience Account; in the event that the Experience Account becomes negative, the insurer will pay the difference, subject to the limits of indemnity.

In the event of a good loss record the balance of the Experience Account, including accumulated investment income, would be repatriated to the insured.

It should be carefully noted that the accounting interpretation of this type of transaction is likely to follow the exact intention or substance of the transaction. For example, the build up of a fund in an Experience Account may have to be recognised as an asset, whilst any future cash (premium) obligations triggered by a claim may be recognised as a full liability. Consequently, and depending on audit approval, the accounting benefit associated with this type of solution may be improving and incremental rather than immediate. Specialist accounting and/or tax advice is essential in this respect.

In addition to meeting the five key concerns, it is important that these structures remain cost-effective compared to the alternatives. On this issue the answer is less clear and depends on the circumstances and particular contracts purchased. In many cases a finite programme may involve higher initial premiums than traditional transfer solutions, but in the event that the contract is profitable (losses are less than premium contributions), then the insurer and insured will share the profits.

As an alternative to fixed levels of pre-loss funding it is possible, dependent upon credit risk associated with the insured, to structure post-loss funding into the arrangement. The objective of this structure is to control the up-front costs in the event of a good loss record and to smooth the impact of exceptionally high losses over time, both from an accounting and cash flow perspective. This leads us on to consider the subject of contingent or committed capital structures.

11.3 CONTINGENT CAPITAL

Contingent Capital is a concept that appears to be gaining some popularity. Contingent Capital is an agreement with a third party to provide new capital to an organisation if a particular set of circumstances occur. A typical contract might include the following points:

- in exchange for a 'small' commitment fee, a third party will agree to provide new capital to a company by purchasing an agreed form of security, for example preference shares, at an agreed price if a major qualifying loss occurs;

- the company will be able to issue the agreed security at any time over an agreed period of time if such a loss occurs;

- there may be certain restrictions as to the continued ability to issue such a security, for example the maintaining of a particular minimum credit rating of the company;

- at the end of an agreed period (using the example of preference shares) the company is contracted to redeem the preference shares at the agreed price. In the event that this does not occur, the coupon rate increases significantly and the shares become convertible. This both encourages the company to redeem the preference shares and provides the counter-party with an element of security.

Contingent Capital structures are emerging as a transparent and efficient way to supplement existing insurance programmes, as well as enhancing flexibility and diversifying sources of capital. In the absence of conventional risk transfer the use of an organisation's financial capacity to cover what might be considered 'remote' risks may be considered inefficient.

One key ingredient to a Contingent Capital structure is the need for a *qualifying event*. Such triggers can be highly customised. For example a trigger could be the presentation rate of claims or alternatively a pre-agreed financial ratio – i.e. operating cashflow or profitability. This helps to structure the solution so that it is meaningful and will react to a situation where value creation is needed.

The type of capital raised (security) can come in several forms including senior debt, subordinate debt, and preference shares. Convertible structures are also possible. Terms can be highly tailored to dovetail with existing bank credit facilities and satisfy rating agency considerations.

The Contingent Capital model allows for a pre-agreed form of capital to be drawn down after a qualifying event. A facility (commitment) fee is paid to secure the facility. In the event of exercising the facility the security would be serviced for an agreed period of time.

The diagram in Figure 11.2 helps to illustrate the concept.

Fig. 11.2

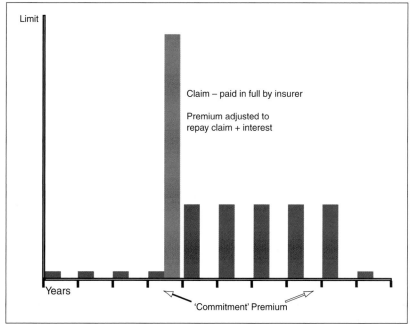

Contingent/Committed Capital Facility

Insurers are uniquely qualified to issue Contingent Capital structures for the following reasons:

- they have an ability to probabilistically assess the 'qualifying event';

- they have a greater ability to structure less conventional instruments which otherwise are not available as a standard in the capital markets or the syndicated bank market;

- they allow insurers to secure diversification benefits.

The advantages to the company of this type of structure is that:

- they provide a facility that will inject new capital into a company at the time when a company most needs it;

- they provide new capital at a pre-agreed cost;

- they allow the company to diversify its capital sources;

- there should be no balance sheet implications until it is exercised and therefore will not affect existing balance sheet ratios.

11.4 OTHER ARF PRODUCT DEVELOPMENTS

Other products give clear pointers as to the way in which future products will develop. These include:

(i)   Loss Portfolio Transfers;

(ii) Integrated Risk Management Policies;

(iii) Dual Trigger Policies;

(iv) Catastrophe insurance using insurance linked securities.

11.4.1 Loss Portfolio Transfers (LPTs)

An LPT structure deals with residual risks of the organisation. They generally are used for employer's liability and public products liability classes. However, in some cases legacy risks such as environmental exposures or industrial disease liabilities, for which anticipated costs can be calculated, can be dealt with. LPTs are useful in order to provide certainty of cost. They can also sometimes take the structure of a finite risk arrangement; however, most structures are for a single, fixed cost buyout price.

LPTs can be used to facilitate an exit strategy for a captive insurance company where the captive has become dormant and is no longer underwriting risk. They can also be used for M&A transactions in order to remove residual risks from the negotiating table.

With an LPT structure the underwriter has to consider its long-term assumption of interest rates and anticipated timing of cash flows. In some cases a time limit may be necessary, as providers may feel uncomfortable in providing unlimited time horizon policy formats. However, the insured needs to be convinced that any such limitation will be acceptable, especially for risks that have a longer manifestation period.

When considering the economics of an LPT transaction, the insured also has to consider the frictional costs of IPT and also the expectation of the security rating of the insurer provider over the longer term.

11.4.2 Integrated Risk Management Policies (IRM Policies)

IRM Policies developed from the premise that financial efficiencies could be achieved by protecting a group or 'basket' within a single structure. In their most basic form this type of arrangement was referred to as a multi year – multi line insurance arrangement. In particular the following arguments were put forward to support the concept:

(a) if the risks within the basket were not correlated, there was no reason why a loss to one part of the basket should cause a loss to another section;

(b) the laws of probability state that the probability of two independent events both occurring within a limited time frame is the product (A x B) of the probability of each event (A and B) occurring in the same time frame;

(c) if the probability of A is, say, 1 in 10,000 per annum and B is 1 in 10,000 per annum, then the probability of both is 1 in 100,000,000;

(d) following (a), (b) and (c) it should not be necessary to purchase catastrophic risk transfer for both A and B. Therefore, buy a single limit for both A and B combined and save premium.

In addition to the above, it was suggested that incorporating unrelated types of risk would create a more stable basket for the insurer, again reducing the risk premium they would charge. In particular, the inclusion of foreign exchange risk and commodity risks was put forward. There have been very few examples of these structures and their success has been mixed.

11.4.3 Dual Trigger Policies

A dual trigger policy pays for the actual losses following two or more simultaneous events. The multiple trigger structure removes the probability of risk, and in some cases enables the insurer to provide genuine risk transfer for risks of a more subjective nature because of the required second, more objective trigger happening.

Dual trigger policies enable a company to consider the required financial value to recover in the event of losses, in the context of what the net financial loss actually means to the company at that time.

11.4.4 Catastrophe Insurance using Insurance Linked Securities

This is a complex area and the student should only be expected to have the briefest of knowledge.

In its most basic form insurance linked securities raise additional necessary risk-taking capital. Most structures have been used in the form of catastrophe bonds (CAT bonds). CAT bonds have been used by insurers to transfer catastrophic risks to the capital markets via a bond issue. Their usage has been associated with hard market conditions where capacity has been limited. A small number of corporates, however, have also used this type of structure. In simple terms a special purpose vehicle (SPV) issues an interest-bearing bond. The SPV may issue an insurance or reinsurance contract to the user for a specific risk category.

In the event of losses the interest payments and/or principal funds may be at risk. The qualifying risk event may be simply a function of an agreed indemnity, with reference to an agreed index (for example a published index of loss estimates) or with reference to a parametric measure, e.g. where earthquake losses are measured against the Richter scale.

Theoretically investors in this type of instrument like them due to their diversification qualities – i.e. natural catastrophe risks are not generally highly correlated with the stock/bond markets.

11.5 THE COMPLEXITY OF ARF SOLUTIONS

The above is a brief overview of some of the general features of ARF solutions. However, by definition, ARF is a bespoke solution and specific structures will be required to pass scrutiny. This will include legal, tax and audit advisers, as well as the treasury and insurance team and their risk advisers who are normally the persons who identify the problem, design the solution and develop contract wordings with the markets.

General Index to
Risk Financing